The Internet and the Language Classroom

Second Edition

Cambridge Handbooks for Language Teachers

This is a series of practical guides for teachers of English and other languages. Illustrative examples are usually drawn from the field of English as a foreign or second language, but the ideas and techniques described can equally well be used in the teaching of any language.

Recent titles in this series:

Teaching Adult Second Language Learners
HEATHER MCKAY *and* ABIGAIL TOM

Teaching English Spelling
A practical guide
RUTH SHEMESH *and* SHEILA WALLER

Using Folktales
ERIC TAYLOR

Personalizing Language Learning
Personalized language learning activities
GRIFF GRIFFITHS *and* KATHRYN KEOHANE

Teach Business English
A comprehensive introduction to Business English
SYLVIE DONNA

Learner Autonomy
A guide to activities which encourage learner responsibility
ÁGOTA SCHARLE *and* ANITA SZABÓ

Planning Lessons and Courses
Designing sequences of work for the language classroom
TESSA WOODWARD

Learner English (Second Edition)
MICHAEL SWAN *and* BERNARD SMITH

Teaching Large Multilevel Classes
NATALIE HESS

Laughing Matters
Humour in the language classroom
PÉTER MEDGYES

Using Authentic Video in the Language Classroom
JANE SHERMAN

Stories
Narrative activities for the language classroom
RUTH WAJNRYB

Language Activities for Teenagers
edited by SETH LINDSTROMBERG

Pronunciation Practice Activities
A resource book for teaching English pronunciation
MARTIN HEWINGS

Five-Minute Activities for Business English
PAUL EMMERSON *and* NICK HAMILTON

Drama Techniques (Third Edition)
A resource book of communication activities for language teachers
ALAN MALEY *and* ALAN DUFF

Dialogue Activities
Exploring spoken interaction in the language class
NICK BILBROUGH

Five-Minute Activities for Young Learners
PENNY MCKAY *and* JENNI GUSE

Dictionary Activities
CINDY LEANEY

The Internet and the Language Classroom
Second Edition

Gavin Dudeney

Consultant and editor: Penny Ur

CAMBRIDGE
UNIVERSITY PRESS

CAMBRIDGE UNIVERSITY PRESS
Cambridge, New York, Melbourne, Madrid, Cape Town, Singapore, São Paulo

Cambridge University Press
The Edinburgh Building, Cambridge CB2 8RU, UK

www.cambridge.org
Information on this title: www.cambridge.org/9780521684460

First published 2000
Second edition 2007

Printed in the United Kingdom at the University Press, Cambridge

Typeface: Adobe Sabon 10/13 pt   *System:* QuarkXPress™   [SE]

A catalogue record for this book is available from the British Library

Library of Congress Cataloging-in-Publication Data

Dudeney, Gavin, 1964–
   The Internet and the language classroom / Gavin Dudeney. – 2nd ed.
      p. cm. – (Cambridge handbooks for language teachers)
   Includes bibliographical references and index.
   ISBN 0-521-68446-3 (pbk.)
   1. Language and languages–Study and teaching–Computer network
resources. 2. Internet in education. I. Title. II. Series.

  P53.285.D83 2007
  418'.0028 5'4678

2006038805

ISBN 978-0-521-68446-0 paperback

Contents

Contents

Acknowledgements

This book is dedicated to Marta, and my parents Peter and Tess. It would not have been possible without the help, support and suggestions of friends and colleagues past and present.

Many thanks too, to Penny Ur, Jane Clifford, Annie Cornford and Frances Amrani for support throughout and making it happen.

The Brief history of the Web activity in Activity 2.1 was first suggested to me by David Hunter. Activity 2.19 was first suggested to me by Paul Henderson, a former colleague. Activity 2.53 was first suggested to me by Robert Campbell of iT's Magazine.

The author and publishers are grateful to the following for permission to reproduce copyright screenshots. It has not been possible to identify the sources of all materials and in such cases the publishers would welcome information from copyright holders.

p.4 The consultants-E; p.7 BBC News screen dump taken from BBC News, www.news.bbc.co.uk; p.11 and 12 screen dumps from Outlook Express. Microsoft product screen shot(s) reprinted with permission from Microsoft Corporation; pp.19, 20 and 23 Google ©Google with permission of Google Inc.; pp.25, 27, 129, 147, 148, 149 and 151 reproduced with permission of Yahoo! Inc. ©2006 by Yahoo! Inc. YAHOO! and the YAHOO! Logo are trademarks of Yahoo! Inc.; p.28 Ask.com UK; p.126 Blogger ©Google with permission of Google Inc., and Graham Stanley; p.127 Wikipedia. Wikipedia® is a registered trademark of the Wikipedia Foundation Inc.; pp.129 and 147 IATEFL.

Overview

This section of the book introduces the teacher to different aspects of the Internet, with a look at software, different modes of communication on the Internet, finding and classifying resources and a brief consideration of some practical aspects of the use of the Internet as a resource bank and as a classroom tool. In this section you will learn how to use the World Wide Web and email, and find information about Interactive Whiteboards.

Activities

This section of the book contains practical activities at all levels, with photocopiable resources and instructions. These include suggestions for procedures introducing and practising Internet use as well as activities on a wide variety of popular themes (e.g. cinema, accommodation, the environment, news and media, etc.) and language points. Many of the activities have sample worksheets and are readily adaptable for most levels.

Tools for Online Work

This section of the book provides sample web-based and email projects including an examination of how to create simple web projects, ideas for extended project work and guidelines on how to set up and run global projects such as email and cultural exchanges. It also considers, albeit more briefly, webquests, blogs and wikis, and online chat.

Teacher Development

This section of the book deals with teacher development online and with the growing area of online teaching itself. It also provides helpful web addresses for you to continue to develop professionally online.

Websites

This section of the book provides a small, quality list of websites to use with your learners. Remember to check the book's own website (http://www.cambridge.org/elt/chlt/internet) for updates to this section and extra material. It should be noted that the Internet is in a constant state of change, and that while all the practical activities have been based around websites with a good degree of stability, it is possible that one or two of the sites mentioned may have changed or ceased to be available by the time you read this. This said, the Internet is such an enormous resource that any website which suffers this fate will surely be replaced by half a dozen more of similar or better quality and content.

The book finishes with a glossary of common terms and a short reading list.

Key

There are various tips and quick 'hands on' activities in most of the sections of this book. Watch out for these symbols as you read:

TIP ☑   **HANDS ON** 🖅

This book includes many suggestions to download, print out and reuse text and graphics from the Net. It is, however, your own responsibility to ensure that any material you find and wish to reuse is free from copyright. Many sites make clear whether or not you have free licence with their material. If in doubt, use the email address to ask them. There is usually one given. Teachers also have a responsibility for child protection, particularly when teaching young learners. When using the Internet, care should be taken about both the kind of material learners have access to, and the type of personal information they publish online.

Introduction

It has now been nearly six years since the first edition of this book appeared, and as I sit here considering what should be included and what should be left out or changed from the original edition, it occurs to me that plenty has changed in terms of the Internet, and the technology we have available to us, yet not much has changed in the way this technology is used, or even in the numbers of teachers actually using it – at least in my experience in teacher training in various locations world wide.

In 2000, Internet connections were slow and costly, and there were, of course, far fewer websites and pages than today: less multimedia, fewer radio and TV stations broadcasting... Clearly, the Internet, or the Net as it is often called, has grown up and has stood the test of time. There can be few people in the world who have not, at the very least, seen a webpage, or sent an email – and few in many parts of the developed, industrialised world who do not use the Internet on a daily basis, either for work or personal reasons.

On the educational side, in my travels for work I have been amazed at how many small towns and villages in rural areas around the world have an Internet café on the main street, used by locals and visitors alike, and reading about elegant wireless education projects in Nigeria or complex online learning ventures in the Amazon in Brazil seems to confirm the fact that the Net has come – or is at least well on the way to coming – of age.

Added to all this, the more recent trend of Interactive Whiteboards and other technological advances have brought both the software and the hardware to a whole new group of educators in all settings and contexts, in a more accessible and meaningful way. Online learning and training, too, have seen incremental growth, with the wide availability of training courses being offered through such free solutions as Moodle and Mambo, allowing even the smallest of institutions to widen its audience and increase its capacity to offer training 'anytime, anywhere'.

Yet despite all these changes in the use of technology and the advances which seem to be spreading quickly through certain sectors of the education world – and despite the fact that the Net is more widely available, cheaper and faster – I still find myself teacher training in language schools and centres around the world where the computers sit gathering dust and the teachers ignore their existence, and I still find myself leading basic computing workshops in these centres.

It remains an unfortunate fact that very little technology training is carried out in our profession, and it is usually up to the individual to find his or her own training – through magazines, books and the Web – so if you're reading this, I hope that you will find the book useful, and wish you good luck in your Internet adventure.

Gavin Dudeney – Barcelona / Krakow, 2006

1   Guidelines

There are hundreds of different ways of communicating by means of an Internet connection, but the simple truth of the matter is that you can get nearly everything you want from the Internet with just two things: the World Wide Web and email. Once you have learnt these two sides of the Net, you will be fully prepared to make full use of all the material in this book.

1.1 The World Wide Web

The World Wide Web (otherwise known as the Web or WWW) is the medium of choice for both new and experienced users on the Net, and for good reasons: it's visually attractive, easy to use, easy to understand, and manages to combine many other Internet-based forms of communication into a single manageable package. It is at once a startling, fascinating, yet somewhat familiar place to be. With its combination of text, images, sound, video, animation, etc., it resembles the kind of multimedia encyclopaedia that you always used to get in a new computer package (back in the days when CD-ROMs were still big news!). If you can manage one of those, then the Web will present no problems.

Most modern computers already come equipped to get connected to the Internet. All you need is a modem, a telephone line (or – for a faster connection – an ADSL modem and ADSL line) and an Internet Service Provider. A modem is a piece of machinery inside the computer, which enables your computer to 'talk' to other computers via a standard telephone line. An Internet Service Provider (ISP) is a company with large and extremely powerful computers, which are permanently connected to the Internet – they are your gateway to the Net. In simple terms, when you connect to the Internet with your computer, you are making a 'phone call' to your ISP: once linked, you can use their computer to gain access to all the other computers connected to the Internet. With an ADSL connection, you have what is called an 'always on' connection, meaning that you pay a flat rate every month and your connection is always available. If you plan to use the Net a lot, an ADSL connection is usually much cheaper and faster than a basic modem connection.

To view and interact with the Web, you use a web browser. This is a piece of software which helps you move around the Web and displays the

3

information you are interested in. There are many different browsers, but the two most popular are: Firefox (or some other flavour of the Mozilla browser) and Microsoft Internet Explorer. Both of these programs are free, and available for both Macintosh computers and the various versions of Windows (Macintosh users might also like to look at Safari).

In the picture below, you can see the Microsoft Internet Explorer browser with most of the major features explained. Firefox is very similar. All the illustrations in this book show Microsoft Internet Explorer. Where there is a major difference between the two, this will be explained.

If you are connected to the Internet, you can get either browser free of charge. To get Internet Explorer, go to http://www.microsoft.com/windows/ie; to get Firefox, visit the Firefox site at http://www.mozilla.com/firefox. If you are not connected to the Internet yet, the best way to get these browsers is to buy an Internet magazine with a cover-mounted CD-ROM – they are nearly always included free. Even if you are connected, but on a slow connection, it's easier and quicker to install them from a CD as the download times for big programs such as web browsers can be long and expensive.

The *Back* and *Forward* buttons let you move between webpages you have visited.

The *Favorites* button shows you a list of all the websites you have saved.

The *History* button allows you to view and go back to the pages you have visited recently.

The *Print* button prints what you can see on screen.

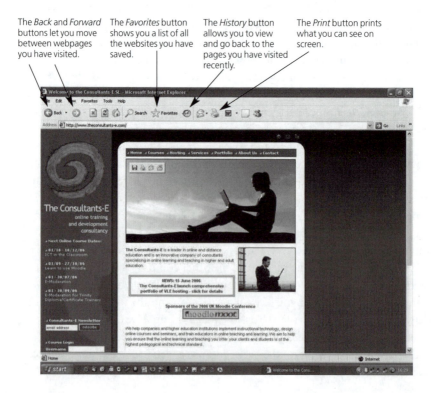

The Web is simply a collection of screens of information (known as webpages), which reside on many thousands of computers around the world, all of which are permanently connected to the Internet. These pages are all linked together, or classified in various directories and search catalogues (the Internet equivalent of the phone directory). When we connect to the Internet, we are gaining temporary access – for as long as we are connected – to these resources.

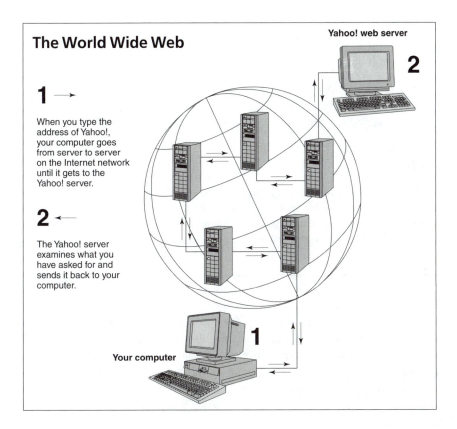

When we visit one of these computers and view something there, we are looking at a website – a collection of webpages built around a common theme. A website can range from a simple page or screen (perhaps an advertisement for, or review of, a book) to an enormous collection of pages (maybe a publishing company's entire book catalogue).

Your first visit

Once you are connected to the Web and you have your browser installed, you will be ready to start visiting websites. To do this, all you have to do is click once inside the white box at the top of your browser window, next to where it says *Address* and type the address of a webpage:
http://www.yahoo.com

This might look indecipherable, but in fact it has a very simple and logical structure:

http://	tells you it's a webpage
www.yahoo.com	is a webpage address – com usually stands for commercial, as does the abbreviation co (see below). Most addresses start with www, but it is also common to see ones without this at the beginning. Note that typing 'yahoo.com' will also get you to the same place.

TIP ☑

You must make sure you type Internet addresses exactly as they appear. If you don't, you won't get where you want to go. Accuracy is everything here – cunning web companies often set up websites with misspelt addresses simply to lure in unsuspecting users, and bad typists!

When you have typed the address, press *Enter* on the keyboard and wait a few seconds. This particular example will take you to Yahoo! – a directory of websites around the world. Here's another example: http://www.telegraph.co.uk

This one will take you to the Electronic Telegraph, the web-based version of the British newspaper *The Daily Telegraph*. Again, you can tell it's a webpage – from the http:// part, and that it's a commercial concern (.co), but you also have the added information, which tells you it's based in the United Kingdom (.uk).

Let's try http://news.bbc.co.uk – the address of the British Broadcasting Corporation's news homepage – I've chosen this one because I'm very familiar with it as it's the first website I visit every day. When you have typed the address, press *Enter* on your keyboard and wait for your computer to go off round the Net until it finds the information you have asked for. When the page appears in your browser window, you will see a combination of text and images:

A homepage is the opening page of a website – rather like the front door to a large house. When you get inside, you can decide which room (or page) you want to visit first by clicking on the links you find on the page.

A link is a word or phrase – or sometimes an image – which is connected to another part of the website using a system called hypertext. These links are usually in a different colour to the rest of the text (usually blue and underlined – but not always) and provide the structure of a website, allowing the user to decide which parts of the site they want to visit.

On the page above there are text links to various sections (on the left) and image links to particular articles throughout the page, next to each article title and summary.

HANDS ON 🖎

Move your mouse over the text and images on a webpage and you will find the cursor sometimes changes shape into a pointing finger – this indicates a hyperlink or connection to another page: click on the link and you will be taken to that page. Try it on the page above.

Notice how the BBC page runs off the bottom of the screen. You can use the scroll bar on the right-hand side of the browser window (or the *Page Down* and *Page Up* keys) to move down and back up the page. Other useful keys for those who prefer keyboards are *Home* – which takes you to the top of a webpage and *End* – which takes you to the bottom.

Try following one of the links and see what comes up. When you've finished looking at the page, press the *Back* button at the top of the screen on the left, to return to the page before. Now try pressing the *Forward* button – no prizes for guessing what it does.

Maybe you've decided that this page could be useful to you later, but how are you going to remember the address? The simple answer is that you bookmark it, like you would an interesting passage in a book. In Firefox, click on the *Bookmarks* button and choose the *Bookmark this page* option – the address will be added to your bookmarks and next time you want to visit this site, you'll simply have to click on the *Bookmarks* button and then click on the name of the site. In Internet Explorer, bookmarks are called *Favorites* and you can create new ones by clicking on the menu item *Favorites* and choosing the *Add to Favorites* option.

Finally, you might think that this site is worth printing out and sharing with other teachers where you work, or taking to class. Nothing could be simpler – simply click on the *Print* button and the page will be printed automatically.

Congratulations! You've learnt almost all you need to know about getting round the Web.

HANDS ON 🖎

Use the list of addresses in the *FAQs* section at the back of the book to practise visiting and moving around websites. Don't forget to add any interesting ones to your *Bookmarks* or *Favorites*. Print a few out to share with colleagues.

1.2 Website FAQs

This is the first of many FAQs in this book. FAQs (Frequently Asked Questions) are often used on websites and discussion lists and their purpose is to answer all the common questions one might ask on a first visit. They are also there to save time for the person who made the website or administers the discussion list!

I'M TRYING TO VISIT A WEBSITE, BUT NOTHING'S HAPPENING. WHAT'S WRONG?

Websites can sometimes be unobtainable temporarily for various reasons. If you try to get to a site and it just won't open – or you get a screen with an error message – first check that you have got the address right. If it still won't open, check your computer is still connected to the server, and try again later. Although some websites do disappear for ever, most of them are fairly reliable.

I CLICKED ON A LINK, BUT IT'S GOING SO SLOWLY. WHAT'S THE PROBLEM?

Connections to the Internet can vary in speed during the day. If a website appears to be taking a long time to get to you, try clicking the *Stop* button on your browser and then clicking the link again. If this doesn't solve the problem, stop and try again later.

I'VE FOUND A GREAT WEBPAGE – HOW DO I PRINT IT?

You can print part of a website by choosing the *Print* option from the file menu and specifying which pages you want to print. If a website is made with frames (multiple windows on the screen) you must first click inside the frame you want to print before choosing the print command. You can print the whole website by clicking on the printer icon at the top of the screen.

WHICH IS BETTER – FIREFOX OR INTERNET EXPLORER?

Everyone has an opinion on which is the best browser. These both do the same things and using one makes it easier to keep track of your *Bookmarks* or *Favorites*. In any case, my advice is to choose one and stick to it.

I'D LIKE TO USE PART OF A WEBPAGE FOR A WORKSHEET. HOW DO I DO THAT?

If you are used to working with a word processor such as Word or similar, you'll find that you can do a lot of work with the two programs open at the same time. Text on a webpage behaves the same as text in a word processor. You can click and drag out a selection of text on a webpage and copy it, then paste it into a word processor document. This is useful for just printing the text from a page rather than all the images and advertisements, for preparing worksheets from webpages, etc. For tips on selecting, copying and pasting text, consult the help file which came with your word processor.

1.3 Email

Once you have had some practice and gained some experience with the Web it's time to move on to look at email. Email is, for many reasons, the most used tool on the Internet: it's easy to use, it's cheap, fast and usually reliable.

Of course, you can use email directly from your browser (Firefox or Internet Explorer), but I really would recommend having an email program apart from your Web browser. There are many reasons for wanting to do this, but the most important one is that a dedicated email program (as opposed to one integrated in a Web browser) works more quickly and more efficiently than the mail service of a browser and is much more versatile, allowing you to work offline and send and receive emails only when connected. This is important for those people paying for their connection by the minute, or for people travelling, in Internet cafés, etc.

TIP ☑

It is worth noting here that as the Internet gains ground in everyday life, the terminology changes. Along with many other people, I use email as one word, but it is still quite common to see it written 'e-mail' – as it was spelt when it was first invented: a short way of saying 'electronic mail'.

Increasingly, the word 'email' is used – and almost universally accepted – as a verb and a countable noun ('I'll email you tomorrow', 'I just got an email from my cousin').

There are many popular email programs, and in the end it's a question of personal preference. The most popular programs are Outlook (or Outlook Express), Eudora and Pegasus mail. In this book I'll be looking predominantely at Outlook, but most of the functions and options are the same in other email packages.

In the picture opposite, you can see a collection of mailboxes on the left-hand side (your Outlook may look slightly different). Notice the most important boxes: the three boxes marked *Inbox* (where messages sent to you arrive), *Outbox* and *Sent Items* (where messages you send go). Other mailboxes include *Deleted Items* (where deleted messages go), *Junk Email*

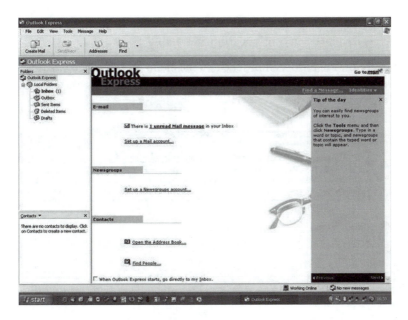

(where spam and other unsolicited messages end up) and any personalised ones you create for filing messages you want to keep.

TIP ☑

Outlook comes as part of the Microsoft Office package, but can be bought separately. If you want to use Outlook Express (and have Windows installed), you should find it already on your computer.

There are normally six steps involved in working with an email program. Most of these steps can be done while you are not connected to the Internet (this is known as working offline), and this is what makes email the cheapest form of Internet communication – you can read messages sent to you, and write new messages without the need to be connected to the Internet and without running up an enormous phone bill.

Here is what you do:

1 Write new mail messages.
2 Connect to the Net.
3 Send the messages and check for new mail.
4 Disconnect from the Net.

5 Read new mail.
6 Reply to mail (then continue from Step 1 above).

To write a message, you simply click on the menu button called *Create Mail* at the top of the screen (keyboard users do Ctrl + N). When you do this, the window below appears:

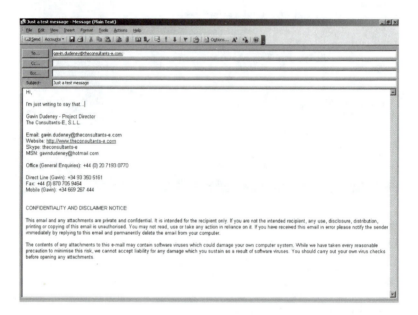

TIP ☑

Because email addresses are difficult to remember, Outlook will automatically remember them for you as new messages arrive, in a temporary location (note that you can also right-click on an email address and choose the *Add to Outlook contacts* option – where you will be able to fill in details of the new contact). If you want to be more systematic about this, click on *File – New – Contact* (Ctrl + Shift + C) and fill in the details, allowing you to add more information about each contact. When you have finished, click on the *Save and Close* button and that person's details will be stored in your Contacts for future use. Next time you write a new message, Outlook will complete the address for you in the *To. . .* field as you start typing the name or address of the person you want to email.

In order to send a message successfully, you need to know the address of the person you are sending to (gavin.dudeney@theconsultants-e.com in the example above). Outlook will automatically put your name and email address in the *From* field. It's customary to put a *Subject* line so that the person who receives it has an idea of what it's about.

Email messages are simply text documents, which can be sent over the Net. They are usually small and written in a 'shorthand' form, ignoring the normal conventions of written language. Essentially this means that they are written in very simple, informal language and there is no need to include the 'extras' of ordinary letters such as dates, addresses or formal greetings. It is not uncommon, for example, to see plenty of abbreviations typical of email communication: 'u' for 'you', 'r' for 'are', and the longer ones such as IMHO (in my humble opinion), FYI (for your information) and BTW (by the way). These are designed to make email quicker to write, and – to some extent – help express feelings and emotions which might otherwise be lost to the reader, or require far more words to communicate. The same is true of 'smilies' or 'emoticons' such as :-) to express a smiling face, or :-(to express sadness.

To write to someone, all you have to know is their address. On the Internet everyone has a unique address and there's absolutely no chance of the electronic postman delivering your message to someone else. My own address is gavin.dudeney@theconsultants-e.com, which sounds something like '*gavin dot dudeney at theconsultants hyphen e dot com*' (the '@' sign is pronounced 'at', whilst the '.' is a 'dot') and means, for those in the know, that my name is almost certainly Gavin Dudeney and that I work at some kind of organisation called The Consultants-E (compare this with the website address: http://www.theconsultants-e.com).

TIP ☑

You have to be very careful when you are writing down email addresses, or typing them into the address field of a new email message you are about to send. One small mistake and the message will be returned to you (just as it often would with a normal letter in real life). This phenomenon is known as bouncing, and it takes up a lot of Internet resources every day. You can do your bit to make the Internet a faster and more efficient place by being careful when sending mail.

When you've finished writing your message, click the *Send* button. The message will be closed and saved in the *Outbox* of Outlook. If you are connected to the Internet, it will be sent immediately and, once sent, transferred from the *Outbox* to the *Sent Items* box. If you are not connected, this will happen next time you connect (but remember, you will need to have Outlook open for this).

When you send your message, it begins a long journey. First it is transferred to the computer of your service provider (the people who give you your connection to the Internet). From there it is sent from computer to computer until it arrives at the computer of the service provider used by the person you are writing to. It waits there until they collect it. Whilst this operation is often carried out in as little as ten seconds, it is possible for it to take a few days if any delivery problems arise. The average time it takes an email message to be delivered is a few minutes.

Messages sent to you arrive at your service provider's computer, where they stay until you collect them. To collect your mail you connect to the Internet, and simply open Outlook. When you do this, the messages are removed from your service provider's machine and moved to your machine, where they land in the *Inbox*. Once you've collected your message you can go offline (disconnect from the Internet) and read them (just double click on any message), print them using the print icon at the top of the screen, delete them (just click once on the message and hit the delete key), or reply to them by clicking on the *Reply* icon at the top of the screen.

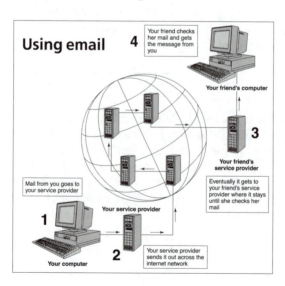

HANDS ON

Try sending some email now. Open up your email program and send yourself a message (this is a good way to see if your mail program is correctly set up). When you have sent it, wait a couple of minutes and then check to see if you have new mail: your message should come back to you in your *Inbox*.

Create a new mailbox called Personal (right-click on *Personal Folders*, choose *New Folder*, type Personal and click OK). Notice how the new mailbox appears on the left of the screen. Right-click on your recently received message, then choose *Move to Folder*, select your new folder (click once on the name) and click OK. Congratulations, you have now filed your message in your new mailbox. It helps to be tidy, especially if you receive a lot of mail every day.

Of course, it's not all fun, and there are rules just as there are for most things on the Net. Short is good – brief messages, shorthand and abbreviations are the order of the day with email. After all, long messages take a long time to transfer and push up phone bills for those people on older dial-up connections who pay by the minute. In addition, some people connected to the Net actually pay for the amount of text they receive, so they will thank you for being brief. The other rules for email and other forms of written communication on the Internet are collected together in a set of guidelines known as Netiquette. Below are a few of the more important issues, but you can find out all about it at the NetManners homepage:
http//www.netmanners.com

TIP

Outlook can automatically add a *signature* to every message you send (e.g. your telephone or fax number, place of work or anything else you want people to know). To create a signature, click *Tools – Options – Mail Format – Signatures*, create a new one and type what you want people to see. Close the signature box and save the changes.

Email can be used for many purposes, from writing to friends and relatives, to having information sent to you on a regular basis (for example the football results every Monday morning, international currency exchange rates every day or even job openings on a weekly basis), to getting hold of resources. It can even be used to send and receive other things such as picture files, documents, sound files, etc.

This particular ability to send attachments is useful for many things. Imagine you want to apply for a teaching job by email. If you copy your beautifully presented CV into an email message, it will lose all its colour, bold text, underlining, etc. since most email does not really support such options. To send your CV as it is, all you have to do is attach it to your email message – this means that it travels with rather than in your message. In Outlook, click *Insert – File* or click on the paper-clip icon and then find and double-click on the name of the file you want to send. Now when you send your message, the file will also be sent to the same address.

You should be aware that the person who receives your message will need the correct software to open the attached file: if your CV was made with Microsoft Word, for example, the person who receives it will need to have something capable of reading Word documents installed on their computer in order to open it.

TIP ☑

If you're not sure what software the recipient has, the best option is to save any document in Rich Text Format (RTF) – you'll find this in the *Save As* dialogue box in programs like Microsoft Word. Just choose the *Save as Type* option and change it to RTF. RTF documents can be read by most modern word processors.

Before sending messages and announcing yourself to the Net world, it helps to practise a little with your chosen email program by writing to friends and relatives. If everything looks fine, you're ready to get out and write to the world.

HANDS ON 📧

Send me some mail. Write to gavin.dudeney@theconsultants-e.com and tell me how you are getting on with the book so far. I promise to answer. Try copying (Cc) the message to yourself, but please don't send any attachments!

If you do not want to use an email program, or your service provider does not supply you with a regular email address, you can still use email via your preferred browser, with one of the free online email services. Not only do these allow you to read and write email inside your browser, but they are also invaluable for those travelling frequently, or for people who do not have connections at home.

Popular web-based email options include:

Gmail	http://mail.google.com
Yahoo! Mail	http://mail.yahoo.com
Hotmail	http://www.hotmail.com

Note that at the time of writing, you need an invitation from a Gmail account holder in order to get an account – this is mostly due to the enormous amount of storage space that Google offers. However, Hotmail and Yahoo! Mail are still free and you can sign up from the addresses above.

1.4 Email FAQs

I KEEP GETTING JUNK MAIL. WHAT SHOULD I DO?

Eventually you will start to receive advertising and 'make money quick' email messages (junk mail). Ignore them: don't waste more valuable Internet resources by replying to them or forwarding them to friends and colleagues. Some email programs (Outlook is a good example) are relatively good at filtering out common junk or spam messages and placing them in a spam folder – it often works fine, but be sure to check that folder for messages which have been misplaced. You can also buy commercial spam filters (try 'googling' for 'best spam filter software').

SOMEONE HAS SENT ME A VIRUS WARNING BY EMAIL.
IS MY COMPUTER IN DANGER?

Don't panic if you receive a virus warning by email. It is impossible (to date) for your computer to be infected by a virus from a simple email message. These warnings travel the Internet constantly and are the bane of experienced users. Again, ignore and delete.

You can, however, get a virus from a file sent with an email message (an attachment) if you open the file. If someone you don't know sends you an attachment you're not expecting, it's safest to delete it if you have no virus protection software.

TIP ☑

Although most virus warnings sent by email are false alarms and hoaxes, there are ways to pick up viruses over the Internet, so it's worth having up-to-date virus protection on your computer – try Norton AntiVirus or McAfee, or the freeware version of AVG (www.grisoft.com).

I JUST GOT A VERY ANGRY MESSAGE FROM SOMEONE I WROTE TO. WHAT DID I DO?

There are a number of things, which offend experienced users of email – here are some possibilities:

- People you write to cannot see your face, or guess what you are thinking. Perhaps you didn't explain yourself clearly, or something in the document was misunderstood;
- Maybe you didn't include information about who you are and where you're from and consequently the person didn't know who the message was from;
- Did you WRITE IN CAPITAL LETTERS? – it's the Internet equivalent of shouting and frowned on by most people;
- It's possible you inadvertently sent an attachment along with your message. Unsolicited attachments are guaranteed to make people angry, especially if they pay a lot for their online time. A teacher I know recently sent a copy of Word for Windows as an attachment – quite by accident – and was very unpopular for a few days!
- Perhaps you have an enormously long signature at the end of your message and the person is angry about the extra time it took to receive your message.

1.5 Searching the Internet

You walk into your local library to look for some information about modal verbs – a simple task in a normal library: go to the languages section, look for books about English grammar, look in the indices of the books under the letter 'M' until you find a reference to modal verbs, then go to the relevant pages. Repeat the process until you find what you're looking for. But what would happen if you walked into the library and suddenly everything had been put in the wrong place? Imagine that there is nobody working in the library, no catalogue of books, and all the books are in disorderly piles on the floor. Suddenly it's not quite as easy as before.

When first approaching the Web, people often feel as if they have just walked into such a library, vainly clicking on link after link, getting nowhere (or worse, getting somewhere which has nothing of interest to them), waiting minutes for large images to appear, attempting to visit pages which no longer exist, etc. After a while any normal person would give up and go back to the newspaper. A familiar comment from new users is that 'there is nothing there', which is rather similar to visiting a hypermarket and commenting on the fact that there was nothing to buy. The fact of the matter is that there is plenty to see on the Web, it's just a case of knowing how to find it, or where to look.

A new user will inevitably be led to one of the bigger search sites like Yahoo! (http://www.yahoo.com) or Google (http://www.google.com), and will try searching for something they are interested in – this search usually involves typing in a word (e.g. Australia) and hitting the *Submit* button. This is what happens if you do just that at Google:

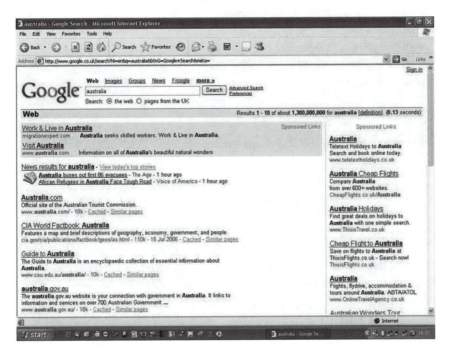

Google has over a thousand million webpages containing the word 'Australia' in its database. It would take years to go through them all looking for something in particular.

With a little refinement, e.g. doing a search for "Sydney Opera House Australia" (the inverted commas are important – see below), the results are dramatically reduced, and in this case amount to approximately 17,600 pages (try it yourself – the first result takes you to the official homepage of the Sydney Opera House).

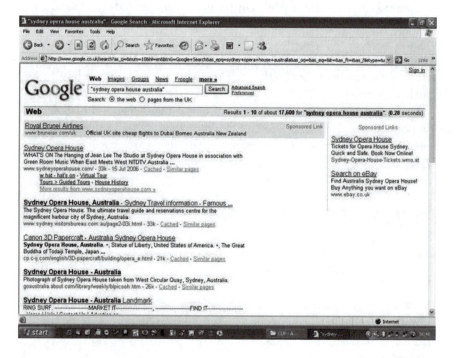

The first results page gives you hypertext links (the blue titles in the image above) to the first ten pages. Each link has a small summary underneath it, and occasional additional information such as the date the page was last changed or updated. If you click on one of the links, you should get to a page which has something to do with Sydney Opera House.

If you scroll down to the bottom of the results page, you will see the words *Result Page* and the numbers 1, 2, 3, … next to it. Clicking on page 2 will take you to the second page of results where you will find links to pages 11–20 of the pages it has found. Eventually, with such small results you should find what you are looking for.

And, every time you actually get to a site you were looking for, use your browser wisely to add the site to your *Bookmarks* (Firefox) or *Favorites* (Internet Explorer). Nothing is more annoying than finding a great site, then forgetting to save a record of its address and having to go through the whole painful process of searching for it again.

I use the word 'painful' with reason: there are no great ways of searching for information on the Web, no guaranteed search processes which will smoothly and quickly take you where you want to go. However, this section of the book will teach you three different ways of searching for resources and hopefully arm you with all the skills you need to find anything you want – albeit with a little trial and error.

Introduction to search types

There are three principal ways of searching the Web: search engines, subject guides and 'real language' search pages.

Search engines allow you to type in words connected with the information you are looking for – these words are then compared with a database of webpages and their contents. Having matched the search words with pages in the database, the search engine displays a list of documents for you to consult. An example of a good search engine is Google (http://www.google.com).

TIP ☑

All search sites have help pages – make sure you visit them and find out how they work – five minutes spent doing this will save many hours and ease the frustration of bad search results.

In the early days of Internet cataloguing, there was only really one contender in the search world, and that was Yahoo! These days, there are hundreds of search sites on the Web, all with different databases, collections, and, of course, webpages. Searching for something on the Web has almost been made more difficult by the proliferation of search sites. But, whichever search site you decide to use, here are some questions you should be asking yourself:

- What exactly am I looking for? (webpage, image, etc.);
- Is this a general or specific search? (general searches work best in a subject guide, whilst specific searches are best left to search engines);
- How much information do I want? (some search agents feature reviews, summary of page content, etc.);

- Can I use the search engine? (some search pages are very difficult to use properly and require a full reading of the help page).

Since it has the biggest database, most people tend to think that Google should be the best search site, and to some extent this is true when we consider a general search. However, a search for 'Apollo 13' on Google will give you far more page references to space technology and disasters than pages leading to reviews of the film of the same name. If you want to find out about the film 'Apollo 13', your best bet would be to search one of the movie databases on the Web (e.g. the Internet Movie Database at http://www.imdb.com). It's all a question of what you want to find – and then working out the best way to find it.

Refining searches using a search engine

As I pointed out in the introduction to this section, visiting a search page on the Web, typing in the word 'Australia' and hitting the *Submit* button will get you a list of millions of sites to visit. Starting this way leaves the user with a wealth of information, and a potential lifetime of investigation on this one subject alone. So just how can a search be refined in order to limit the number of page references returned? The answer lies in the shape of 'operators' and punctuation. Let's see what these tools are:

TIP ☑

Google can search for webpages in most languages. If you are looking for resources in Spanish or French or a language other than English, try changing your *Preferences* at the top of the Google screen.

AND, OR AND NOT

These look for various combinations of search words and operate like this:

AND

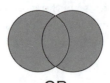
OR

NOT

- **AND** (+) looks for documents featuring **all** words in the search entry box;

- **OR** looks for documents featuring **any** of the words in the search entry box;
- **NOT** (-) looks for documents featuring **some** words, but not others.

Therefore a search for *EFL **AND** London* should take you to sites connected with teaching English as a Foreign Language in London, whereas a search for *EFL **NOT** London* will find you all the sites on the subject anywhere else in the world. A search done using *EFL **OR** London* should give you a list of both types of site (and a lot more).

TIP ☑

Some search engines use the words 'AND' and 'NOT', others use the mathematical symbols '+' and '−'. To find out which ones to use on a particular search engine, read the help file. Google will do all this for you from the *Advanced Search* page.

These three search words can be 'nested' (i.e. combined), providing very close matches: *EFL **AND** London **AND** (study **OR** teach)*. That is if you're looking for information about studying or teaching English in London.

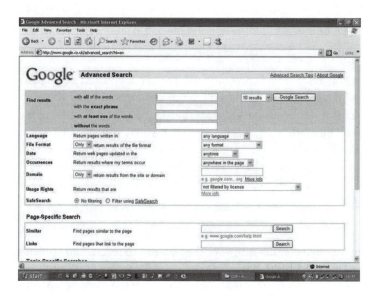

Notice the options: 'with **all** of the words' is the equivalent of using AND, 'with the **exact phrase**' is the same as enclosing your search in inverted commas, 'with **at least one** of the words' is the same as a random search for all the words separately, and '**without** the words' will exclude any words typed in that particular box (NOT).

HANDS ON 📧

Try going to the Advanced Search page of Google and doing some searches using the options described above. See if you can find the address of my personal homepage, not my business one, which was given earlier in this section. Gavin is not the most common name in the world, but you won't want to find all the Gavins.

If you don't have too much luck, you'll find the address towards the end of this section of the book.

Note: These search terms are taken from the world of mathematics and are sometimes referred to as Boolean Operators. If you see this term anywhere on the Internet, just think AND, OR and NOT.

PUNCTUATION

Punctuation (as the word is used in the context of a search site) allows the user to look for phrases (or parts of phrases) in Web documents. This is probably the most common way of searching. Punctuation in this context refers to the use of inverted commas.

When you use inverted commas you have to put yourself in the place of the person who wrote the page you are looking for. Let's suppose you are looking for some information about Marilyn Monroe for a class about famous people – if you made a page about her, what would you include? (pictures, biography, filmography, etc.) So, you could start with a search along these lines: *"biography of Marilyn Monroe"*. The words have to occur next to each other, and in that order as part of a phrase to score a hit with the search.

TIP ☑

Using inverted commas is one of the best tips to teach your students. One of my students in Barcelona once tried searching for "the Sting's biography," instead of "biography of Sting" – a common mistake for Spanish learners of English. He didn't find anything, but he soon learnt not to make the same mistake in English!

Search strategies for subject guides

Subject guides have more in common with the index of a book, with information classified by topic, subject, etc. These allow users to browse through lists of sites by subject, in search of something relevant. The main difference between these and search engines is that subject guides are compiled by humans. This has both a positive and negative effect on searches: positive in the respect that the database for the search engine usually only lists top-level documents (homepages) and therefore doesn't take you to the middle of a website; negative in that the database is usually a lot smaller than that of a search engine (humans being slower than machines!). An example of a good subject guide is Yahoo! http://www.yahoo.com

---

TIP ☑

There are many different versions of Yahoo! for different countries. Follow the links from the homepage to the Spanish Yahoo!, the German Yahoo!, the Japanese Yahoo!, etc.

Yahoo! can also be used as a search agent in much the same way as Google – you can use the operators AND and OR, and even quotation marks from the *Advanced Web Search* page. However, its real strength lies in its structure: that of a Subject Guide:

HANDS ON 🖅

Visit Yahoo! now and browse some of the sections (Yahoo! Web Directory near the bottom of the homepage). Try to find webpages connected with your hobbies and interests, or look for information on a famous person. Now try the same thing in Google based on what you have read above. See how quickly you find what you are looking for.

Yahoo! allows users simply to browse through categories and sub-categories, gradually refining a search until the desired results are achieved. A typical search, which might take a considerable amount of time on Google can often be a lot quicker through Yahoo!.

Searching for resources on Yahoo! can be considered like an inverted pyramid: you start with a wide area of reference and keep refining it and making choices until you get where you want to be. For example, if searching for a biography of Sting for a class on pop music, a typical route might be:

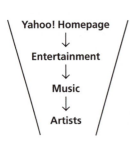

Starting at the homepage, first click on the *Music* sub-heading of *Entertainment*. When this page has opened, click on *Artists*.

If we go back to the idea of a library, this is similar to finding the right area and shelf before beginning the search for a particular book.

Once you get to this section of Yahoo! type 'Sting' in the search box and select the '*this category*' option before searching (see opposite).

Now we can search for Sting, but just in this category. This restricts results to Sting the musical artist rather than the other stings (jellyfish, nettle, wasp, bee), which we may have got if we had searched from the Yahoo! Homepage.

TIP ☑

While writing this I was asked by a colleague to help her find the website of *The Scotsman* – a newspaper published in Scotland. Here's how the same search works on Google and Yahoo!:

Google
Searching for *The Scotsman* brought back just over 13 million results – the first of which was a direct link to the homepage of the newspaper. This took a couple of seconds only.

Yahoo!

Searching from the front page for *The Scotsman* brought back 14 million results – the first link was to a portal page connected with Scotland in general and the second link was direct to the home page of the newspaper. The site displayed advertising to the right of the main search results. Another option was to follow links through *News – Newspapers – By Region – Countries – United Kingdom – Scotland*, which also got me a direct link to the newspaper at the top of the page.

Using 'real language' search sites

Using search facilities like Google and Yahoo! is not for everyone. Even when you know all the different ways of searching, it's sometimes a very time-consuming process to get to what you are actually looking for. Wouldn't it be nice if you could just ask something like 'Where can I find a picture of Sydney Opera House?', just like you would if you were asking a colleague, or visiting the ideal library we were considering earlier.

The answer is that these days you can. All you need to do is Ask (http://www.ask.com). Ask is a very simple way of searching the Net. You don't have to remember all the advanced rules of pages like Google and Yahoo! – you just type in a normal question and see what happens.

'Real language' search pages are the human side of searching the Net. They allow the browser to ask a question, then they give suggested answers. Like Google, Ask features an enormous database of websites and pages, yet the user doesn't have to remember any of the intricacies of Google, it's enough just to ask your question and consider the answers proposed by Ask. However, don't expect incredibly precise results all the time – computer programs just aren't very good at being intuitive yet.

Having said that, if you try it out a few times, you might be surprised at the excellent results you can get. This might all seem very magical, but in actual fact Ask is only doing what the other two search pages do, it just does it in a more user-friendly way. Ask doesn't actually understand real English, so when you type a question like: 'What time is it in Bangkok?' the only words Ask recognises are *time* and *Bangkok* – it's good to know, but don't tell your students as it's great practice for them in forming correct questions using Wh- words, punctuation, etc.!

HANDS ON

You can Ask all sorts of questions. Try some of these examples taken from the Ask help pages, then try some of your own and see how accurate the results are:

- How many albums did Miles Davis make?
- How can I make chocolate cake?
- How tall is the Empire State Building?
- Where can I find photos of cats?
- Why is the sky blue?
- Who is the prime minister of Ghana?

You might be asking yourself why you should bother with the other ways of searching the Net when this seems to be so much easier. The simple answer to that is that there is no one single, complete database of all the pages on the Web – each search engine has different records, and there's a good chance that if you can't find it through one engine, you'll find it through another. It really does help to use a variety of approaches.

It's also worth bearing in mind that a search engine is not always the quickest way to find things; some of the bigger sites such as the Microsoft one (http://www.microsoft.com), the BBC (http://www.bbc.co.uk) or the Encyclopaedia Britannica (http://www.britannica.com) have enormous amounts of useful information.

TIP

Ask has an excellent partner site called AJ Kids. It only looks for pages and websites which are for kids and which are guaranteed to be free of 'adult' content. It's a great site to take younger learners for an introduction to the Internet.

Visit AJKids at http://www.ajkids.com

Making search choices

We've looked at three search engines here, and I went through a lot more of them while preparing this. The conclusion has to be that no single Web search system is really 'the best'. None of them includes all of the Internet in its database. Google and Yahoo! are often considered to be the best, but as we have seen here, they both have their good and bad points. It's a case of experimenting until you find the right results. If you don't find what you're looking for with one of the three we've looked at here, have a look at this list of further search sites. But remember, as soon as you get to one of these pages, read the help file.

MSN Search	http://search.msn.com
Looksmart	http://search.looksmart.com
Lycos	http://www.lycos.com
Altavista	http://www.altavista.com
AllTheWeb	http://www.alltheweb.com

1.6 Search FAQs

HOW DO I FIND IMAGES OR LINKS TO SPECIFIC PAGES AND SITES?

Google features the possibility to search for a certain portion of a document (an image, a title, etc.). Try <*allintitle:"The Electronic Telegraph"* > to find pages with the phrase The Electronic Telegraph in the title. <*link:news.bbc.co.uk*> matches pages that contain at least one link to a page with news.bbc.co.uk in their address. Use the *Images* search on the main page to find images only. See http://www.google.com/help/operators.html for more details.

WHY AREN'T MY SEARCHES WORKING WELL?

If you find you're getting no search results when you use AND and NOT, try using the mathematical symbols '+' and '-' instead. Depending on the search engine, these are used in place of the words. As I've already pointed out, the first thing you should do when you visit a search page is find out exactly how it works.

WHY AM I GETTING SO FEW RESULTS?

A recent survey of search engines found that they are fast falling behind in their efforts to catalogue the Internet, and that Google – usually considered the biggest in terms of how many pages it has in its catalogue – is only aware of an extremely small percentage of the total content of the Internet. I always recommend starting with either Google or Yahoo!, but it's worth bearing in mind that just because you don't find what you're looking for on one of these two pages, it doesn't mean that it isn't out there somewhere. Sometimes you'll have to use a selection of search pages before you find what you're looking for.

HOW DO I FIND TEACHING MATERIAL AND WEBSITES?

It's worth bearing in mind that if you are looking for something connected to teaching, another teacher will already have done the same thing, so a good way to find it is to use the network of online teacher groups and discussion lists (see *Section 4*) and teaching websites (which follows) to help you out.

1.7 The Internet as resource bank

With these search techniques, and contact with other teachers through email, you should be getting pointers to great resources on a regular basis, and this should really be giving you some idea as to just how much useful material there is out there. Before we move on to the last part of this section in which we'll be looking at some considerations of using the Internet in class (as opposed to using material from the Net in class), here's a quick word about saving a little time when looking for foreign language resources in particular.

As teachers have been working with the Net for quite some time now, they have both developed their own sites full of useful material, and come across many others made by colleagues around the world. If you are looking for useful foreign language sites, it makes sense to see if anyone else knows where they are before setting off on a journey through Google, Yahoo! and Ask. With this in mind, here are a couple of starting addresses where you will find a lot of links to language resources on the Net.

Dave's ESL Café: http://www.eslcafe.com
Apart from having plenty of useful sections itself, Dave's ESL Café has an enormous collection of links to EFL resources on the Web. It's a big site, so make sure you have a lot of spare time before digging under the surface.

its-online: http://its-online.com
its-online is a web-based magazine full of excellent lesson ideas, discussion pages and links to resources in many categories.

A visit to these two will give you links to more than enough sites of interest, and they are shortcuts through the dense information forests represented by major search engines.

> **TIP** ☑
>
> There are plenty of links to these and other resources in *Section 5* of this book. By the time you read this, some of them may have disappeared. For an updated list of useful links, check the website which accompanies this book at: http://www.cambridge.org/elt/chlt/internet

1.8 The Internet as a classroom tool

More and more schools these days have study centres or rooms equipped with a quantity of computers, often connected to the Net. In fact, any school which has a handful of computers can very easily and cheaply connect them to the Internet. Not only does this make it easier for teachers to gain access, but it also gives them the opportunity of introducing students to it as well. This opens up a world of possibilities as far as teaching goes, from giving students access to the 'world knowledge' they often don't have, to putting them in touch with other students of the same language around the world, taking part in collaborative projects on a global scale, to sending their homework to their teacher by email.

But all this technology can also spell disaster in the wrong hands, or in the wrong circumstances. This section is a brief look at some of the considerations involved in using computers and the Internet in schools and some tips to follow for a smoother experience. The last part of this section introduces the Interactive Whiteboard and considers how this is impacting on classroom use of the Net and other technologies.

> **TIP** ☑
>
> If you teach a lot of business or in-company classes, there's a good chance that the companies where you work will have computers connected to the Internet. Use these to take advantage of some of the excellent corporate websites and business publications on the Net. (See *Section 5* of this book.)

Before you take your students along to do any class based around the Web or email, you should be very sure that you know the technology yourself. Hopefully, if you have gone through *Section 1* so far, and have spent some time experimenting with the Net, you'll be feeling confident enough to introduce your students to it. Remember, apart from introducing your students to the Net, you may also be introducing them to basic computing skills as well. Before you start them on any kind of structured class, make sure they know how to start and shut down the computers, how to run a program, even how to move the mouse round the screen, point and click. However you do it – and you may find that you want to combine it with basic word processing skills – you must make sure that they are relaxed and unafraid to try things out (see **Section 2** for class plans dealing with first classes using computers and the Internet).

An Internet class needs to be as well planned and structured as any other class. You must go through the material in advance and make sure that the language, content and presentation are what you want for your class. In addition to all these considerations, there are some other skills and points – perhaps not quite the normal language teacher preoccupations – which need to be taken into account.

Access to computers

In an ideal world we would all be working with enough computers to go round. But in reality, it is rare for there to be one Internet-connected computer for every student in the class. As a general guide, one computer per three students works well for most Internet class activities, with each student taking a turn at 'driving'. For email penpal exchanges, one between two is better, and both students can be occupied at the same time by one dictating as the other types. Actually, even when enough computers are available it is often a bad idea to have one student per computer as this tends to discourage or inhibit conversation.

The archives of TESL-L (http://www.hunter.cuny.edu/~tesl-l/) have plenty of resources and records of past discussions dealing with ideal classroom layouts and classroom management techniques. Below are two sample computer room layouts and considerations of their advantages and disadvantages.

Layout one has students working on a central table, with the teacher at the end equipped with a whiteboard and an overhead display of what s/he is doing, for students to follow. This has to be a reasonably big room with a table which allows for enough space between computers for books, dictionaries, etc. The biggest disadvantage to this layout is the fact that students cannot readily see the people opposite them.

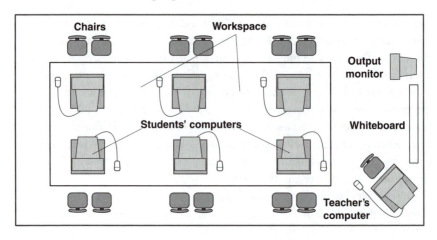

Layout one

Layout two has students working round the outside of the room, then swinging in on their chairs to work together with books, dictionaries, etc. and to get instruction from the teacher. Whilst this layout provides a clear break between computer time and time spent on other activities (and stops people 'fiddling' when the teacher wants more control), it is difficult for all students to see the teacher at any given time, especially when they have their backs to the classroom space.

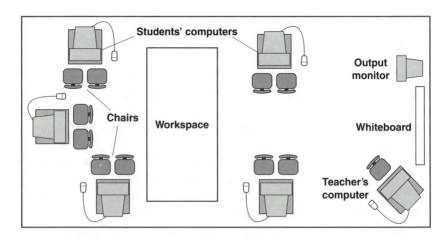

Layout two

Speed of access

Internet access can be very slow at certain times of the day, from certain
locations around the world, and due to certain types of connections or
connection sharing. It's important to know this, as it can help you prepare
for your classes better. If, for instance, you are going to do a class which
involves lots of multimedia elements such as video clips and sound files, it
makes sense to download them in the morning, and save them on your hard
disk. Later, when you need to use them, you won't have to rely on having a
fast connection because they will be stored on your computer.

To save (rather than view online) a multimedia file such as a video or
audio selection, click on it with your right mouse button and choose the *Save
target as ...* option, then choose a directory on your computer and click OK.
Remember where you save it!

Page caching

Both Firefox and Internet Explorer perform a function called caching. What
this means is that when you visit a website, all the pages and images are
automatically stored on your hard disk. These pages are stored for a certain
amount of time (specified in days), or until they reach a certain size (in
megabytes). You can change these settings to suit your browsing habits –
check out *Tools – (Internet) Options* in most browsers to alter them.

When you go to a website, the first thing your browser does is see if it has
the site saved in its cache – if it does, it displays it instantly. Then it goes and
has a quick look at the original site to see if anything has changed – if that is
the case, it updates the changed elements. If it can't find the site at all in its
cache, it will perform its usual job of retrieving it from the Internet.

What this means to you is that if you visit the sites you want your students
to visit just before the class starts, they will all be saved in the cache. When
your students return to these sites a short while later, they will all come up
much quicker than if they had to go and get them over the Net. Inevitably
your students will want to branch out and visit sites you haven't stored in the
cache, but even a little preparation helps.

I have found that explaining to students that the Net can sometimes be
slow is enough for them to be understanding. In any case, the excitement of,
and interest in, the Net is often enough for students to have far more
patience than you will.

Website life

There is little point planning an Internet class around a particular website unless you are sure that the site in question has a good pedigree and has been in existence for quite some time. Whilst most professional websites are reliable and long-lasting, you may find the perfect site for a class, only to discover three days later that this site no longer exists. This usually only happens with personal homepages, but it has been known to happen with larger sites. The secret is to find two or three sites which deal with the same theme, leaving the lesson plan adaptable. Then if the site that you really want to use is not working, or has disappeared, you'll always have a back-up.

TIP ☑

Most personal homepages have this symbol ~ somewhere in their address: http://www.xtec.es/~bferran

This symbol often doesn't appear on the keyboards of users outside the US. To make it, hold down the *Alt* key and type *126* on the numerical keys on the right of your keyboard. When you finally take your finger off the *Alt* key, the symbol will appear.

Technology breakdowns

And while we're on the subject of back-ups, it's worth bearing in mind that any class which revolves around technology needs a back-up plan for when the machinery breaks down, or there's a power cut. Using the Internet is a little like using a video player – if the player doesn't work, or the cassette gets stuck, there really is no way round the problem. At least with an audio cassette there is always the possibility of reading the text aloud, but just as it would be impossible for a teacher to try to recreate a scene from a film, there is very little you can do with a broken connection to the Net, or a set of websites which refuse to download. Again, a little forewarning of your students will avoid a large part of the disappointment, should the situation arise.

Keeping control

There is no really simple solution to controlling access to programs in an open environment like a school. If you must do it you have to choose between password-protecting the whole system or using software which requires user identification before running a program. A quick look at these options will explain why they are generally more trouble than they are worth.

Start-up password

With this option, the computers cannot be turned on without someone typing in a password. This provides very good security, but also reduces the accessibility of the machines, making it necessary for the person who knows the password to be present every time they are turned on. As anyone who works with computers a lot will know, they often crash and stop working when you least expect them to, and if you have to keep asking for the password to be entered every time this happens you will quickly find this inconvenient.

Custom software

These mostly prohibit access to particular programs as defined by the person in charge, using combinations of usernames and passwords. They can be very effective as long as the password is not given to too many people. Again, though, people will share their passwords, forget them and find countless other ways of making this a troublesome procedure.

Having examined both of these options, I have to say that I am more in favour of relying on users' innate sense of responsibility, and on the assumption that there will always be a member of staff 'on duty' to control access to programs and Internet material.

This, coupled with a minimal installation of non-vital software (games, hardly-used applications, etc.) and an up-to-date anti-virus package usually proves sufficient. If you keep the number of programs installed on your computers to a minimum, and provide protection against viruses, you'll find your computer use should be reasonably trouble-free.

'Questionable' content

Whenever we see an article about the Internet in a newspaper or magazine, on the TV or radio news, the focus is often on the 'fact' that the Internet is a potentially dangerous environment for young people.

While there are some sites which should be avoided, they are not nearly as prevalent as the press would have us believe. However, if you are using the Net with young or adolescent students, you should be aware that they could get access to materials which are not suitable for the classroom, and that it's your job to 'police' their activities whilst accessing information.

There are two ways to approach this problem – the software approach and the practical approach:

The software approach

This software usually works in one of two ways:

1 Pages are checked for a certificate issued by a 'recognised' authority before they are displayed. These certificates indicate what kind of content the pages have, and the audience it is suitable for. If the pages have a certificate and the content is deemed suitable for the person browsing, the page will be displayed. If there is no certificate, the program blocks the site and a warning is issued.
2 Pages are checked for words in a database (these are generally connected with sex, violence, racial issues, etc.). If any of them are found, the page is not displayed and a warning is issued. These databases generally come pre-configured with a set of words to which it is possible to add your own.

If you feel that you really do want to install software of this kind, you might like to take a look at the following products:

• SurfWatch
• Net Nanny
• CyberPatrol
• CyberSitter

They all do more or less the same job using one or both of the methods described above – but the results are never exactly what you would like, and can be more restrictive than really useful. With varied standards and different ways of 'grading' sites, it really is a hit-and-miss approach.

The conclusion has to be that censorship is a weighty matter, even when it does work, and with the plethora of standards currently under consideration, it becomes almost impossible to implement intelligently and with little fuss or negative impact on your teaching and your access to information. My own opinion is that common sense and a trust in people, along with good training and education will almost always ensure a fruitful and decent use of the facilities you make available to people.

The practical approach

There are a number of measures, which you can take to ensure that your students are using the equipment as they should:

1 Make sure students realise that this is a facility, which should be used, appreciated and not abused.
2 Make sure you're the only one to set passwords on anything.

3 Scan the hard drives regularly for *.gif and *.jpg images (the most common formats for images from webpages). If you suspect someone of downloading pornography or similar, check for new pictures after s/he has used the Internet.

4 Configure email programs to reject messages over a certain length, thus cutting down on the chance of someone having undesirable pictures and material sent to them by mail. Ask your technical staff or a friendly computer expert to help you with this.

5 Watch out for people giggling nervously over the other side of the room. Equally, notice whether the computer always suddenly crashes and needs to be re-started when you appear.

6 Check the Firefox Cache and Explorer Temporary Internet Files directories for suspect files (see Page caching above).

7 Always have someone on hand to supervise Net access.

There is a fine line between supervising and patrolling. Knowing how to walk that line is important. Most users won't even bother with the murkier side of the Net, but a firm warning of what is and what is not acceptable will do more good than an immediate ban.

Recent developments

Recent developments in learning technologies seem to have shifted the focus from individual or pair work with computers to more collaborative group classes and activities. This has been particularly noticeable in the arena of Interactive Whiteboards (IWBs, or Smart Boards), which combine computers and Net connections with data projectors to project an interactive image onto a specially prepared electronic version of the traditional whiteboard.

Described by *The Guardian* (http://education.guardian.co.uk/getonboard/ 0,16957,1679885,00.html) as '*a ground-breaking tool*' that is '*providing pupils with a new learning experience and presenting teachers with an opportunity to involve young people as never before*', IWBs are still in their relative infancy and offer few ready-made resources for the English teaching world to date.

Essentially, the computer and Net connection become a shared resource, always available to the class on the whiteboard. Teachers and learners can use the whiteboard to show content from CD-ROMs and the Internet, and this content can be annotated, illustrated, saved and printed. They can be used in this way, as an ad hoc resource, in most situations. More principled use, however, will require much more careful planning on the part of the teacher.

Of course, IWBs can also be used exactly the same way as an ordinary whiteboard, except that you don't need pens and erasers since the electronic tools perform the same function. The advantage here is that anything written can be stored and recalled for later use.

EFL materials publishers have joined this new technological revolution, with recent coursebooks featuring IWB-ready materials, which further exploit the more traditional coursebook materials often in a more active and engaging way. Interactive exercises allow learners to drag words and chunks around the board, building up sentences and mini-dialogues in a more interactive way and listening material can be finely controlled by each individual learner, etc.

What has become apparent, as a result of the little research that has been done so far, is that IWBs appear to be a good way to introduce other forms of technology in the classroom – and to reduce technology fears often experienced by educators – by using a much more familiar interface than many other tools available. Essentially, the whiteboard is something that most teachers are extremely familiar with, and are therefore more comfortable using.

The potential for this kind of tool is enormous in terms of sharing content in the classroom, and for offering students access to a wider pool of knowledge than can traditionally be offered otherwise. However, it has been pointed out that IWBs tend to promote a much more 'heads-up' and lockstep approach to teaching and learning and this trend has been widely criticised in some circles. It remains to be seen whether these tools will go the way of the multimedia CD-ROM, or will survive the test of time.

If you are lucky enough to teach in a centre that has IWBs and have not yet had the opportunity, time or training to try them out, you may like to take a look at Graham Stanley's blog on the subject: http://iwb-efl.blogspot.com/ where you will find plenty of commentary and ideas for exploiting them with your learners.

Activities

This section introduces practical activities by theme and level. These activities take the teacher from the most basic introductory classes through a wide variety of popular themes (e.g. cinema, accommodation, the environment, news and media, etc.). Many of the activities have sample worksheets and are readily adaptable for most levels. Most of these activities were designed for use 'live', i.e. in a study centre equipped with computers connected to the Internet. If you are not in that position, you can still – with a little judicious printing, or some clever use of even one computer connected to the Net – use the great majority of them.

Activities by level

Some activities marked for students of Business English may not be explicitly designed for this purpose, but the themes and websites lend themselves to a simple adaptation for this field.

Young learners
2.1, 2.2, 2.5, 2.19, 2.25, 2.26, 2.29, 2.34, 2.37, 2.38, 2.41, 2.42, 2.47, 2.50, 2.55

Elementary
2.19, 2.23, 2.25, 2.29, 2.34, 2.37, 2.38, 2.39, 2.41, 2.42, 2.43, 2.47, 2.50, 2.55

Lower-intermediate
2.1, 2.2, 2.5, 2.8, 2.13, 2.15, 2.16, 2.18, 2.19, 2.23, 2.28, 2.34, 2.37, 2.39, 2.43, 2.50, 2.53, 2.55

Mid-intermediate
2.1, 2.2, 2.5, 2.8, 2.11, 2.12, 2.13, 2.15, 2.16, 2.18, 2.19, 2.21, 2.23, 2.27, 2.28, 2.31, 2.34, 2.35, 2.37, 2.39, 2.44, 2.49, 2.50, 2.52, 2.53, 2.55

Upper-intermediate
2.1, 2.2, 2.3, 2.4, 2.5, 2.7, 2.8, 2.9, 2.10, 2.11, 2.12, 2.13, 2.15, 2.16, 2.17, 2.18, 2.19, 2.20, 2.21, 2.22, 2.23, 2.24, 2.27, 2.28, 2.30, 2.31, 2.33,

2.34, 2.35, 2.36, 2.37, 2.44, 2.45, 2.46, 2.49, 2.50, 2.51, 2.52, 2.53, 2.54, 2.55

Advanced
2.1, 2.2, 2.3, 2.4, 2.5, 2.6, 2.7, 2.8, 2.9, 2.10, 2.11, 2.12, 2.13, 2.14, 2.15, 2.16, 2.17, 2.18, 2.19, 2.20, 2.21, 2.22, 2.23, 2.24, 2.27, 2.28, 2.30, 2.31, 2.32, 2.33, 2.34, 2.35, 2.36, 2.37, 2.40, 2.44, 2.45, 2.46, 2.48, 2.49, 2.50, 2.51, 2.52, 2.53, 2.54, 2.55

Business English
2.1, 2.2, 2.4, 2.6, 2.7, 2.10, 2.11, 2.16, 2.19, 2.21, 2.24, 2.28, 2.33, 2.35, 2.37, 2.49, 2.50, 2.54, 2.55

Activities by theme

This classification describes the principle theme of each activity.

Advice: 2.3, 2.4
Animals: 2.43
Art: 2.36
Astrology: 2.22
Biography: 2.7
Books, reading: 2.17
Celebrations: 2.38
Cinema: 2.12, 2.31
Clothing: 2.34
Colours, shapes: 2.47
Computers, Internet: 2.1, 2.2, 2.26, 2.49, 2.55
Countries, nationalities: 2.29, 2.47
Describing people and things: 2.7, 2.22, 2.23, 2.24, 2.34
Entertainment: 2.44
Famous people: 2.6, 2.7, 2.8, 2.18, 2.36, 2.46
Food and drink: 2.25

Games, puzzles and quizzes: 2.37, 2.50
Holidays and travel: 2.14, 2.19, 2.20, 2.28, 2.30, 2.35, 2.38
House and home: 2.33, 2.48
Inventions: 2.54
Language: 2.15, 2.16
Logos: 2.21
Music: 2.5, 2.18
Mystery: 2.42, 2.45, 2.48
Names: 2.53
News: 2.10, 2.11, 2.41
Personality: 2.22, 2.23
Shopping: 2.32
Sport: 2.27
Survival: 2.51
Teenagers: 2.3, 2.52
Time: 2.29
Television: 2.13
World problems: 2.40

2.1 Introduction to the Net (I)

Aim:	To introduce basic Internet skills and concepts
Focus:	Vocabulary connected with computers and the Internet
Level:	Lower-intermediate and above
Time:	60 minutes
Sites:	http://www.google.com
Notes:	This activity is designed to introduce students to the basic skills they will need for the other activities in this section.

Procedure

A simple questionnaire about computing habits is a good introduction to
this activity. Make sure to include discussion questions about the Internet:
has anyone used it? (at home / work / school?) What have they used it for?
What is it for? What can you find on the Net? You will find a sample
below. When they have finished talking, get feedback and general reactions
to the subject. Then try the *Brief history of the Web* vocabulary activity
below.

Show students how to open a web browser, type in an address and go to a
website (try Google as a good starting page). Give students a printout of the
web browser window with the Google main page in it. Go through the
various functions of a browser (see *Section 1* for a reminder) and let students
make notes and label their printout. Allow students time to play with Google
and encourage them to find a website connected with a hobby or interest
(don't forget to show them how to *Bookmark* or add *Favorites*!). When they
find a page show them how to print it out. When they have finished make
sure they know how to exit the browser and leave the computers tidy for the
next class.

Put students into groups and give them time to compare their printouts
and talk about the pages they have found. Discuss the process they have just
been through and deal with the issues which usually arise – speed, content,
etc. (See *Section 1* for more information.)

Follow-on

If you have good access to the Internet, give students more time on Google
and get them to prepare a presentation on a hobby or interest using pages
they find.

Computing habits

Have you got a computer at home? What do you use it for?
Do you use a computer at work / school / university? What for?
What do you know about the history of the Internet?
Do you use the Internet at home, at work? What do you use it for?
Which of the following can you use: chat, instant messenger, Skype, a webcam . . .
Have you ever bought anything on the Net? If so, what?

© Cambridge University Press 2007

Brief history of the Web

**Read "The Web Story" and put the correct form of the words in the gaps.
One example (*address*) is done for you.**

Personal computers (PCs)	Small computers which people use at work/home.
A network	Computers joined together so that they can communicate.
The Internet	A network of millions of computers around the world.
Electronic mail (email)	A way of sending and receiving messages on the Internet.
The World Wide Web	A user-friendly way of looking at words or pictures and listening to sounds on the Internet. Also called the Web or the WWW.
A browser	Computer software used to look at the Web.
A site	A place on the Internet, also called a webpage.
An address	The location of a site/webpage.

The _____ has existed since 1969. It was created by the USA military as a way of communicating even after a nuclear war. Universities soon used it. At first it was only used to send and receive _____ messages. Thirty years ago computers were very big and very expensive. Today millions of people use computers at home and at work. Many people can afford to have a _____ at home and, at work, computers are joined over _____s. In 1991 _____ was invented. Now people looked at words, saw pictures and even heard sounds from around the world on their PCs. The Web was very popular. In 1987 there were 10,000 webpages but by 1992 there were more than one million _____s and many millions of webpage **addresses**. Thirty years ago a few people used the Internet to send email. Today, all you need is a PC and a _____ like *Explorer* to discover the wonderful world of the Web.

© Cambridge University Press 2007

2.2 Introduction to the Net (II)

Aim:	To introduce Web searching skills
Focus:	Question forms
Level:	Lower-intermediate and above
Time:	60 minutes
Sites:	http://www.yahoo.com http://www.google.com http://www.ask.com
Notes:	Your students will often want to find specific information on the Internet. This activity teaches them how to search using different search pages. Note that the *Trivia quiz* used to introduce the activity will need to be adapted to suit your group.

Procedure

Use a trivia quiz like the one below to generate interest. How well can your students do? It's a good idea to include some questions they are certain to be able to answer without using the Net as well as some they probably won't.

Introduce students to the different ways of searching using Google, Yahoo! and Ask (see *Section 1* for a reminder) and give them time to practise with the three sites. In groups, students try to finish the trivia quiz you've given them. When they have finished, give them some time to search for things they want to look at. The sample quiz below can be shortened to fit the time available, or you might like to try giving students a limited time to answer as many as possible, then pooling results to see if the class as a whole has managed to answer all of them.

In groups, students prepare a trivia quiz for their colleagues to do. This is a good opportunity to do some work on question forms. When the quizzes are ready, students can have a quick return visit to the Internet to practise their newly-acquired search skills.

Follow-on

When the *Trivia quiz* has been done, students can prepare a similar quiz for you to try. In multinational groups, each country can be represented by a question for you to answer.

Variations

This activity can easily be adapted for younger learners by substituting the search sites for Yahooligans! (http:// yahooligans.yahoo.com), Ask Kids (http://www.ajkids.com) and Lycos Kids (http://www.lycoszone.com).

Trivia quiz – searching on the Web

1 What was the name of the 23rd president of the United States?
2 Who invented the aspirin?
3 How many players are there in a basketball team?
4 What's the capital of Australia?
5 What's the weather like in Paris today?
6 How many albums have the Rolling Stones recorded?
7 What product is Jamaica famous for?
8 Which film won the Oscar for Best Picture in 1996?
9 Who was the first person in space?
10 Who wrote *One Hundred Years of Solitude*?
11 Who is the prime minister of Poland?
12 What is the current number one single in the UK?
13 How many American dollars (US$) make 10 Euros (€)?
14 What's the top news story in Australia today?
15 Where is Manitoba?

Use any of the search pages to find the answers you don't know.

© Cambridge University Press 2007

2.3 Giving advice

Aim:	To look at teenage problems and giving advice
Focus:	Revision of functions for giving advice, reported speech
Level:	Upper-intermediate and above
Time:	60 minutes
Sites:	http://www.teenadviceonline.org – archive section

Procedure

In groups students talk about and list the kinds of problems they have (or had) as teenagers. What advice were they given? What happened in the end?

Divide the class into two groups and put the titles of some of the problems from the Teen Advice Archive on the board (make sure the problems are suitable and that the language used is what you want to focus on in the class). Each group should have about four titles. Give them time to decide what they think the problems are about, who they think is involved and what advice they would give the people.

Introduce them to Teen Advice and give them time to find the problems you gave them in the Archive. They should go through the problems and see if they guessed the content correctly. Ask them to make notes on the problems and advice given, and also write down any language for giving advice that they find.

Divide students up across the two groups to tell each other about the problems and advice they looked at, and ask them to compare the language for giving advice that they found. Put the language on the board.

Follow-on

There are plenty of good traditional activities for this kind of language work, including 'running counsellors' where half the class are counsellors and the other half have problems (nothing too sensitive). Students with problems have a minute with each counsellor to explain their problem and get advice. At the end of the activity, votes are cast for the best counsellor.

Other options include a writing task where students are writing a case report on one of the problems, detailing the person and their problem, and the advice they were given – and making use of reported speech. Finally, why not try a class magazine (either on paper or as a web project – see *Section 3*) with a problem page?

TIP ☑

The suggested site features many problems dealing with sensitive areas. Make sure you read through the problems you are going to use thoroughly before looking at them in class. You could also look at: www.lucie.com and http://www.student.com/askadvisors.php

---

2.4 I've always wondered …

Aim:	To find out things you've always wanted to know
Focus:	Direct and indirect questions
Level:	Upper-intermediate and above
Time:	60 minutes
Sites:	http://www.askanexpert.com

Procedure

Start the class with the *It's a mystery* activity below. Give them time to think and complete the sentences, then get students to walk around asking questions to find someone who can answer the things they've written. When they've had time to get as much information as they can, discuss the possibility of finding the information on the Internet. Where would students look? If they've done the search activities in *Activity 2.2 Introduction to the Net (II)*, they should have a good idea.

Introduce students to the Ask an Expert site and give them time to look around for the people who might be able to help them. Some of the experts just have links to their websites where they say you should look first before contacting them personally by email, others have direct email links. If students can't find the answers to their questions, try the Ask site. When they find answers to their questions, they should make notes. This is a fascinating site, so allow some time for exploration.

Students get into groups and swap interesting or unusual information they have found.

Follow-on

You could prepare a set of questions such as: 'Why is the sky blue?' or similar and get students to walk around as above. If students don't get their answers from other students or from the Ask an Expert page they could try searching Ask Jeeves (http://www.ask.com) for the relevant information. A good follow-on is to do a class project on the town or city where you work: 'Little-known facts about …'.

Another good follow-on activity is to walk around while students are using the Internet and make a note of the best, most interesting or most unusual questions which students have been able to find an answer to. If you work quickly you can make a 'Find someone who …' activity for later in the class (or the following lesson): take half a dozen of the things students have found an answer to and produce a quick questionnaire to distribute around the class (e.g. 'Find someone who … can explain why the sky is blue', 'Find someone who … knows how to make a paper aeroplane' etc.). Students can then walk around the class asking questions until they find the answers, then noting the name of the person who supplied the information.

TIP ☑

There are no guarantees that students will find answers on the suggested sites to the questions they write. If this is the case, encourage them to use search engines to find the rest. See also http://www.ehow.com/

It's a mystery

Complete these sentences.

1 I'd love to know . . . .
2 I've always wondered . . . .
3 I've no idea why . . . .
4 Why do you think . . . .?
5 Have you any idea . . . .?
6 Does anybody know . . . .?

© Cambridge University Press 2007

2.5 A song class

Aim: To prepare songs to present to the rest of the class
Focus: Vocabulary connected with music
Level: Lower-intermediate and above
Time: 60 minutes
Sites: http://lyrics.astraweb.com   http://www.lyricsworld.com

Procedure

In pairs, use the *Talking Music* discussion sheet below to start the activity.
Get some feedback and do a song activity of your own. These invariably lead
to a discussion between teacher and students as to what constitutes 'good
music'. Tell them they are going to have a chance to get their own back by
preparing a song class for everyone else to do.

Introduce students to the International Lyrics Server site and show them
how to search for lyrics. Once they have found the lyrics to a song they
would like to do in class, demonstrate how to select the lyrics (*Edit – Select
All*) and copy them (*Edit – Copy*). Open up a word processor and paste the
lyrics into a new document (*Edit – Paste*). Now get the students to use
Yahoo! (see *Activity 2.2 Introduction to the Net (II)*) to find a photo of the
band or star whose song they have chosen – this is best accomplished by
going to the Entertainment/Music/Artists section and searching from there.
When they have the lyrics and the photo together in their word processor,
make sure they save the document and print it out.

Each group who has found a song is in charge of producing a song
worksheet. Help them decide what they want to do (e.g. gap-fill, re-arrange
words, correct the mistakes) and give them time to produce a finished

worksheet. These can be used throughout a course with each group presenting and 'teaching' their song.

Follow-on

Using Yahoo! students could also find biographical information on the band they have chosen. This could then be turned into a presentation or project, or even a website (see *Section 3* for details).

Talking music

In groups, discuss the following questions:

1 Who are your favourite pop stars and bands?
2 What are your top five favourite albums of all time?
3 What is the best song ever recorded?
4 What's the best music video you've ever seen?
5 What's the best concert you've ever been to?
6 Do you prefer mp3s, cassettes, mini discs, CDs or vinyl records?
7 Which bands or pop stars do you dislike?
8 How much money do you spend on music per month?

Find out anything else you would like to know about your group's music habits.

© Cambridge University Press 2007

2.6 20th century news

Aim:	To review the 20th century
Focus:	Past tenses, used to, descriptions
Level:	Advanced
Time:	75 minutes
Sites:	http://www.pathfinder.com/time/time100/index.html

Procedure

The Time site divides the people of the 20th century into five categories: leaders and revolutionaries (politics), artists and entertainers (the Arts), builders and Titans (business), scientists and thinkers (science) and heroes and icons (society). Put the five categories up on the board and brainstorm people to go in each category. Time has twenty in each section, so aim to get at least five from the class.

Give students the opportunity to look at the names of people in the five categories. Who are they surprised by, and who is missing, in their opinion?

Divide the class into two groups and get them to choose one person from
each section, making sure they know a little about them and that they have
an opinion as to why they should be chosen as the winner in their particular
category.

Each group introduces their chosen winner in each category, giving a
brief description of their life and achievements and saying why they should
win. At the end of the presentations, the class votes for a winner for each
section.

Follow-on
There is a lot more to do at this site. Other features include the Time Warp
section which compares 1900 to the end of the 20th century – useful for past
tenses and structures such as 'used to' and 'didn't use to'. There is also a 20th
century quiz (Test Your Knowledge) and other fun sections such as Event of
the Century and 100 Worst Ideas. These could be used variously for
comparisons, prediction exercises, etc.

2.7 Heroes hall of fame

Aim:	To look at the heroes and heroines of modern life
Focus:	Describing people, past tenses, present perfect tense
Level:	Upper-intermediate and above
Time:	90 minutes
Sites:	http://pathfinder.com/Life/heroes/hall.html

Procedure
Start this activity with a pyramid discussion. Individually, students make a
list of their ten heroes or heroines from both the past and present. Then in
pairs, they discuss, compare and negotiate to make a list of ten from their
twenty. Two pairs get together and repeat the process. The negotiations
continue in bigger groups until the whole class has agreed on ten.

For a shorter activity, try brainstorming the names of heroes and heroines
directly onto the board. Have a class discussion on who the ten most
important ones are, and why.

Students visit the Life Hall of Heroes and look at the list to see if any of
their heroes appear. In groups students choose three heroes they don't know
and have a look at their biographies, making notes. They then get into bigger
groups to compare what they have found. Women are sadly missing from the
Hall of Heroes – how did they do in the students' lists? Are women less likely

to be appreciated than men? The Distinguished Women of Past and Present site (http://www.distinguishedwomen.com) has famous women divided up into categories (when searching choose the *Field of Activity* option). Brainstorm famous women as a class activity then allow students to look around. Who did they forget?

Get feedback on what students have seen using the *Famous but forgotten?* activity below.

Follow-on

In a single nationality class, you might like to look at how many people from that country figure in the Hall of Heroes – if there aren't any, brainstorm famous people from the country. In mixed nationality classes, the same can be done, with students telling the rest of the class who their national heroes are.

Other possible follow-ons include a visit to http://www.biography.com for some games and puzzles in the famous person quiz or anagram game. Another good site for general information on famous people is the Famous Birthdays site at http://www.famousbirthdays.com where students can see who shares a birthday with them. This is also a good opportunity for students to do a written assignment on a famous person from their country. For help in writing a biography, they could have a look at the Biography Maker – a guide to how to write a good biography – at http://www.bham.wednet.edu/bio/biomaker.htm. This also makes an ideal topic for an extended project or website (see *Section 3* for details).

Famous but forgotten?

What did you think of the Hall of Heroes site – were you surprised by the content?
Who do you think was there, but shouldn't have been?
Who do you think should have been there, but wasn't?
Who are the heroes and heroines from your country?

What do you think the criteria should be for being famous?
If you could be famous, what would you like to be famous for?

© Cambridge University Press 2007

2.8 Celebrity dinner party

Aim: To find out about famous people
Focus: Past tenses
Level: Lower-intermediate and above
Time: 60 minutes
Sites: http://www.celebsites.com   http://www.yahoo.com

Procedure

For this activity you'll need some pictures of famous men and women (living or dead). Try to find a selection of scientists, politicians, pop stars, actors and actresses, writers, etc. Display the pictures and elicit any information the class knows about the people. If you lack the time or resources to prepare an activity like this, simply provide the names of celebrities, or perhaps have a quick quiz, with you providing surnames and the class providing the first names as you write them on the board.

Explain that the class has won a competition to host a celebrity dinner party and that they can invite four of the people shown.

Use the sites suggested or, alternatively, give students a chance to practise their search skills. In pairs, they have thirty minutes to find out about the people they are not familiar with, and make some notes on their achievements and reasons for being famous. When they have finished, they should be in a position to decide who to invite.

Give everyone a seating plan and give each pair a chance to arrange their guests around the table in such a way that everyone will have somebody interesting to talk to. Then put pairs together to discuss their arrangements and explain who they have invited and why. They should also be encouraged to say why they have people sitting next to each other, and where they themselves would sit and what they would like to ask their guests.

Follow-on

There are plenty of opportunities to adapt and extend this activity. Students might like to plan the menu for the evening (are any of the celebrity guests vegetarians?) or perhaps arrange an interview with their favourite guest. The interview can then be written up.

TIP ☑

Current celebrities can be found at the CelebSites website. For older famous people, dead ones or the scientist / politician / writer range, use Yahoo! sections. This can also be adapted for Business English classes, using appropriate figures from the world of business, finance, etc.

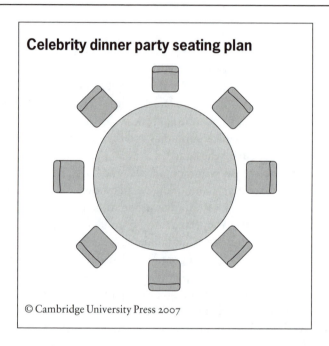

Celebrity dinner party seating plan

© Cambridge University Press 2007

2.9 The weather

Aim:	To talk about weather and extreme weather conditions
Focus:	Weather vocabulary, describing the weather, numbers, facts and figures
Level:	Upper-intermediate and above
Time:	60 minutes
Sites:	http://www.weather.com/encyclopedia http://weather.yahoo.com

Procedure

Start with some work on the various ways of talking about the weather (it's sunny, the sun is shining, etc.). Brainstorm vocabulary to complete the grid below. With lower level classes, you might like to provide them with the

vocabulary they need to complete the grid and have students classify it
according to the headings:

Destructive	Serious	Noteworthy	Normal
tornado	....	boiling	warm
....	....	....	....
....	....	....	....
....	....	....	....

© Cambridge University Press 2007

Divide students into As and Bs and give them either five mythical people
(Zeus, Thor, Jupiter, Indra and Helios) or five historical figures (Cleveland
Abbe, Anders Celsius, Gustave Coriolis, Daniel Fahrenheit and Evangelista
Torricelli). They then visit the Weather Channel's Storm Encyclopaedia and
find out as much as they can about the people they have been given, and
what their connection is to the weather. As and Bs then get together to
discuss what they have found out. The Storm Encyclopaedia has plenty of
different sections for different types of weather. Give students a chance to
visit these (flooding, heatwave, etc.) to complete the vocabulary grid they
started earlier.

Get feedback on the information about the people and correct the
vocabulary grid.

Follow-on
This lends itself nicely to a typical newspaper disaster headline and story, if
you can find some pictures of tornadoes, floods, etc. Pass round the pictures
and put some headlines like the following up on the board: *Floods Leave
French Farmers Fuming / Canadian Catastrophe Catches Careless Campers
Catnapping / Twister Tears Town Apart*. Have a close look at the headlines
and brainstorm some possible facts and events related to each one before
leaving the students to write the final article. You might also want to discuss
unusual weather events that your students remember in the last year or two,
maybe widening it out into extreme conditions such as earthquakes,
tsunamis, etc.

Another fun activity is to use webcams – cameras connected to the
Net – to find out what the weather is like at the moment. Visit
http://www. www.weatherimages.org/weathercams/ for details.

2.10 **Strange news**

Aim:	To discuss recent news stories
Focus:	Telling stories, anecdotes, conversational skills
Level:	Upper-intermediate and above
Time:	60 minutes
Sites:	http://news.yahoo.com

Procedure

Get some topical cartoons or news headlines from newspapers and magazines and pass them out in groups. Students try to remember (or guess) what the stories were. Can they remember anything curious or funny which has happened recently?

Divide the class into groups and give each group three or four headlines from the Odd News section of Yahoo! News Headlines. Can they guess what the story is? They make predictions as to what they think each story could be about. You can also do a vocabulary prediction exercise – which words would they expect to find in each article?

Students visit the Yahoo! News Headlines site and find their stories. They then read them and make notes on them.

Later students get into bigger groups – or as a whole class activity – and tell each other their stories, including new (and useful) words they have learnt.

Follow-on

You could take a look at some language used for swapping anecdotes: 'This is a great one …', 'This one's funny …', 'I've never heard that one before …', etc. There are also plenty of Urban Myth sites on the Net (a quick search of Yahoo! or AltaVista will turn up quite a few), which can easily be exploited in this context.

A writing activity where students write the article, based on strange headlines you provide is also a good follow-on.

I have found this to be an excellent quick activity for higher level students. Not only is it a lively and interesting start to a class, it is also an invaluable source of vocabulary.

TIP ☑

The stories at the Yahoo! headlines site change regularly, so it is not a good idea to choose your headlines too far in advance. This activity is

---

an ideal one for doing entirely offline if necessary. The Yahoo! news site also features business news.

2.11 Making the news

Aim:	To design the perfect newspaper
Focus:	Vocabulary connected with the news
Level:	Intermediate and above
Time:	60 minutes
Sites:	http://www.crayon.net

Procedure

You could start with the *In the news* activity, getting feedback and general opinions on what is and what isn't considered interesting to your students. Alternatively, brainstorm some vocabulary connected with newspapers (e.g. broadsheet, tabloid, headline, article) and their different sections.

Put students into groups and get them to design the perfect newspaper – they should discuss the following criteria and agree on final details. They should think about:

- The title of the newspaper;
- The newspaper's motto (e.g. Tomorrow's News Today!);
- The sections it would have, and their order.

Crayon allows people to create their own newspapers, complete with title, motto and sections. The news which then fills this paper is taken from free Internet news sources. Students simply fill in a form at the website and submit their newspaper. They are then given a unique web address where they can consult their newspaper daily. Crayon automatically updates the different sections on a daily basis, so once the newspaper has been designed it will always be up-to-date.

Students can compare and talk with other groups about the newspapers they have designed. This can then lead on to a discussion about the quality and content of newspapers available locally.

Follow-on

One excellent follow-on is to introduce the idea of a class or school magazine or newspaper which can either be done in the traditional way or as a website (see *Section 3*). Another follow-on is to bring in examples of real newspapers in the language you are teaching and allow students to have a look through them.

TIP ☑

This can also be used with Business English classes as a good warmer, with students dipping into their newspaper before or at the start of class.

In the news

In groups, talk about your preferences and reading habits:

- What newspapers and magazines do you read?
- Do you read a newspaper every day? And on Sunday?
- What are your favourite sections of a newspaper?
- What sections do you never read?
- Do you read your horoscope every day?
- Do you read the cartoons?
- What would your ideal newspaper have in it?

© Cambridge University Press 2007

2.12 Film reviews

Aim:	To write and publish film reviews
Focus:	Vocabulary connected with movies and the cinema
Level:	Mid-intermediate and above
Time:	90 minutes
Sites:	http://www.imdb.com

Procedure

Use the film reviews sheet to start off the activity. Get feedback and then brainstorm vocabulary connected with films (types, people involved, etc.). Get students to write the name of a favourite film on a piece of paper and give it to a partner – the partner then has to get as much information as possible by asking relevant questions. Each partner should make notes about the film as they are talking.

Visit the Internet Movie Database and give students time to look at the reviews section, noting how each review can have lots of different parts. You might want to prepare a quiz along the lines of: *Who was the leading actress in Wuthering Heights?* etc.

When students have a good feel for the personal reviews which are submitted to the site they can start to plan theirs. Get them to look back over the notes which were made for them earlier and begin to flesh them out until they have a complete film review. Correct and encourage re-writes and peer critique until the reviews are good enough to submit to the site.

Follow-on

This would be a good opportunity to do a video session with your class. You can find useful back-up and preparatory material at Hollywood Com http://www.hollywood.com. Another useful site for preparing film sessions in class is The Internet Movie Script Database http://www.imsdb.com

---

TIP ☑

The Internet Movie Database is the biggest movie resource on the Net. There is no guarantee that film reviews submitted to the Internet Movie Database will actually ever appear on the site. If this is likely to cause disappointment you might like to consider turning this into your own website (see *Section 3*).

Film reviews

Think about your views on the cinema, then talk to a partner:

- What sort of films do you like?
- When was the last time you went to the cinema?
- Who are your favourite actors and actresses?
- Do you prefer the cinema or watching videos?
- What are the best and worst films you have ever seen?

© Cambridge University Press 2007

2.13 Square eyes

Aim:	To talk about television / decide what to watch
Focus:	Television vocabulary, agreeing and disagreeing, giving opinions
Level:	Lower-intermediate and above
Time:	75 minutes
Sites:	www.bbc.co.uk www.itv.com www.channel4.com – listings section

Procedure

Hand out copies of a local newspaper's TV page. Ask students to go through the listing and make a note in English of the different types of TV programmes they can find (e.g. documentary, soap opera). Feed in vocabulary as necessary, then get feedback as a group. Give out the *Viewing habits* questionnaire and pair students off to talk about and compare their views on TV.

Tell students they are going to have a quiet night at home in front of the TV (6 pm to midnight, for example) and that they need to find something to watch. Give them time to look at the different websites and decide what they are going to watch. They should make notes of times, descriptions and channels.

Start off with pairs or small groups and give them time to negotiate and agree on a viewing schedule. With lower level groups you may need to do some pre-teaching of structures used for agreeing / disagreeing and giving opinions. When they have agreed on what they are going to watch, combine two groups and repeat the process until the whole class has agreed on what to watch that night.

Follow-on

Written programme reviews are a good follow-on activity, with students watching a programme and writing a short review. With higher levels, English-language newspapers usually have good TV review pages which can be used for exemplification or as a starting point (or try http://www.ciao.co.uk/TV_Programmes_8711_3).

This is also an ideal opportunity to do some work on the 'opinion' style of writing task where students are asked to state the case for a particular issue such as *TV is nothing but sex, violence and repeats.*

TIP ☑

This activity can be done with TV listings from any country which has a selection of channels. Although this uses British TV pages, it is easily adapted for most countries since the majority of TV companies now have online schedules.

Viewing habits

1 How many hours a day do you spend watching TV?
2 What types of programmes do you watch?
3 What types of programmes do you never watch?
4 What's your favourite programme?
5 Do you watch a soap opera? Which one?
6 What did you watch last night?
7 Do you watch 'serious programmes' like the news, documentaries, etc.?
8 Do you watch the adverts?
9 Do you ever video any programmes?
10 Describe the perfect evening of TV for you.

© Cambridge University Press 2007

2.14 Eco-tourism

Aim:	To plan and report on exotic holidays with an ecological slant
Focus:	Past and future tenses, holiday vocabulary, experiences
Level:	Advanced
Time:	90 minutes
Sites:	http://uk.tickle.com/test/traveller/start.html http://www.responsibletravel.com/TripSearch/Ecotourism/ActivityCategory100020.htm

Procedure

Use the *Holidays past and future* activity to start this class. Get feedback on the discussion, introduce the idea of eco-tourism and find out if anyone has ever had a holiday like that. See if students can think of parts of the world where this might take place. Brainstorm vocabulary for activities, places to stay and the kinds of things you would have to take with you on such a holiday.

Students visit the Tickle site and do the What Kind of Traveller Are You? quiz. Then visit the Responsible Travel site and divide students up into different destinations. Each destination has photos, activities, itineraries and a section on how the holiday makes a difference. Get them to work through their holiday, making notes. Then as a whole class compare and discuss, and decide on a final location to go on holiday.

Students now create a tour of their country for adventurous travellers, advising them on where they should go, and what they should see and do on the holiday. In mixed nationality classes, students could bring photos and information from their countries to do a presentation in a follow-on class.

Variation

A slight variation would be to divide the class into groups of potential travellers and travel agents. Travel agents then prepare by looking at the holiday descriptions whilst travellers prepare a set of questions they want to ask about possible holidays.

Follow-on

The Responsible Travel pages also include holiday reviews. This is a good opportunity to work on story-telling techniques, and an ideal opportunity to introduce a writing activity.

Holidays past and future

In groups, talk about your holiday experiences and wishes.

- What's the best holiday you've ever had?
- What's the worst holiday you've ever had?
- Who do you like going on holiday with?
- Do you prefer an active or a lazy holiday?
- What do you pack when you go on holiday?
- Which countries have you visited and which would you like to visit?
- If you were very rich, what would you do on holiday?
- Where would you never go on holiday?

© Cambridge University Press 2007

2.15 A little *Je ne sais quoi*

Aim:	To learn about borrowed words in English
Focus:	Foreign words and expressions used in everyday English
Level:	Lower-intermediate and above
Time:	45 minutes
Sites:	http://www.krysstal.com/borrow.html

Procedure

Hand out copies of the **Borrowed words** quiz and give students a little time to match the words and countries. Get some feedback on their decisions, but don't go over the correct answers yet.

Get students to go to the Borrowed Words website and find the words from the quiz, noting where the words came from. Quick finishers can have a look around this page and find out if there are any words in English which have been borrowed from their own language. This is an ideal opportunity to teach students how to search for something on a webpage – click *Edit*, then choose *Find (on this page)* and enter the word you're searching for, followed by a click on the *Find Next* button. This will significantly cut down the quantity of reading involved.

Get feedback on the correct answers. Now brainstorm the activity in reverse, with students thinking of a list of English words which are used in their own language. Do equivalents exist in the original language? The worlds of technology, food and music are particularly rife with English words.

Follow-on

With higher level groups, a discussion about 'language purity' works very well – with students tackling issues such as the evolution of language, 'inventing' new words, etc. With lower level groups, a map of the world can be used to practise country names and languages, with countries also being illustrated with a word which English has borrowed.

Borrowed words

Match the words used in English on the left with the language they came from originally:

1	ketchup	A	Inuit
2	robot	B	Japanese
3	paper	C	Hungarian
4	igloo	D	Amoy (Chinese)
5	yeti	E	Turkish
6	walrus	F	Czech
7	paprika	G	Tibetan
8	karate	H	Polish
9	yoghurt	I	Egyptian
10	horde	J	Norwegian

© Cambridge University Press 2007

KEY: ketchup – Amoy / robot – Czech / paper – Egyptian / igloo – Inuit / yeti – Tibetan / walrus – Norwegian / paprika – Hungarian / karate – Japanese / yoghurt – Turkish / horde – Polish

2.16 The same language?

Aim:	To find out about US and UK English
Focus:	American and British English variants
Level:	Lower-intermediate and above
Time:	60 minutes
Sites:	http://www.englisch-hilfen.de/en/words/ae-be2.htm

Procedure

Take ten American English words which are different in British English. Easy words include: drug store (chemist), gasoline (petrol), pants (trousers), cab (taxi), elevator (lift), store (shop), mad (angry), french fries (chips), sidewalk (pavement) and trunk (boot). Put them into sentences to add some context, e.g. 'Your room is on the seventh floor, Sir. You have to take the elevator.' or 'Please join the line to buy tickets for the next show'. Give students some time in pairs to look at the sentences and try to decide what the British English equivalents are.

The website has two-way conversion (i.e. British to American and American to British). Give students time to find out if they have the right conversions. Now hand out the *What did you say?* activity and give them time to convert it to British English. Get feedback and correct where necessary.

Variations

This activity works both ways, so if you teach predominantly American English, you can easily change the focus of the tasks. This activity can open up into an extended discussion on the differences in English around the world, and whether British English or American English is more predominant in the countries where the students come from. For lower levels, try replacing the *What did you say?* activity with a set of pictures representing the different things.

TIP ☑

This is one of many sites dealing with the difference between American and British English, and one of the better ones since it doesn't 'take sides'. You can also try http://esl.about.com/library/vocabulary/blbritam.htm and be sure to check out the quiz at: http://iteslj.org/v/e/ck-british-american.html, which is a fun way of following up this activity.

What did you say?

James from London is on holiday in America. He's having problems with some of the vocabulary. Can you help him do the shopping?
'Well James, it's good to have you here in New York finally. Can you run out to the store and get some food? I haven't had time. OK, here's what we need . . .

. . . a few packets of potato chips for the party. You'll have to go to the liquor store, too, and get some beer. Then we also need some cheese and bread, and get some cookies and candy for the kids. We don't want everyone to be hungry.

OK, then we need to eat tomorrow. Can you get some ground beef – we can make stuffed eggplant with fries or baked potatoes. Get some dried fruit, too – you need to go to the health food store for that. Oh, and get some bread and jelly for breakfast.

I think that's everything – thanks a lot.'

© Cambridge University Press 2007

2.17 A good book

Aim:	To talk about reading habits
Focus:	Vocabulary connected with books and reading
Level:	Upper-intermediate and above
Time:	90 minutes
Sites:	http://www.amazon.com

Procedure
Start with a vocabulary brainstorm on books, reading and reading habits. Pre-teach any of the words from the *Are you a bookworm?* activity which you think might cause problems (e.g. blurb). In pairs, students do the activity. Get feedback as a class and discuss general reading habits.

The Amazon.com Best Sellers Paperback Fiction section has news and reviews of current paperback bestsellers. There are short reviews of the top-selling novels of the moment and reviews from members of the public who have liked and disliked them. The task for each student is to find a novel for the person they talked to during the preparation stage, and one for themselves. They should then get back into their original pairs and explain what they have chosen and why.

Follow-on
Prepare some colour photocopies of book covers for students to look at, but try to remove any blurb or information about the books themselves. If you

can't prepare these yourself, use a selection of books from home or the library, but limit access to the front cover only.

Go over the different parts of a standard book blurb, taking a real book as an example, or perhaps using one from the Amazon site. This usually includes: a short summary of the story, reviews from newspapers, comments about the author, etc. Students have to look at the covers of the books, select one that inspires them and create the blurb, including some or all of the parts.

For very high levels, the 'first line' game can be fun. Take a selection of books and give one to each student. In turn, each student reads out the blurb from their book and then copies out the first line of the book onto a strip of paper. Everyone else writes what they think the first line might be. When everyone has finished, the student collects all the first lines (including his or her original one) and reads them out. Students get five points for guessing the correct first line (i.e. the original), and they also win ten points from each student who thinks the one they wrote was the real one.

Are you a bookworm?

Ask your partner these questions:

- Not including textbooks, how many books do you buy a month?
- How do you choose a book: by the cover, the blurb, the name of the author or something else?
- What is your favourite type of book?
- Where do you usually read: in bed, on the train, in the bath …?
- Do you have a favourite literary character or hero?
- Do you ever use a library, or do you prefer to buy books?
- Do you have a favourite author whose books you always read?
- Do you prefer to see the film first and then read the novel or vice versa?
- What was the title of the last novel you read? Who was the author?

© Cambridge University Press 2007

2.18 Ladies and gentlemen ... The Beatles

Aim:	To find out about famous Beatles songs
Focus:	Talking about famous people, biographies
Level:	Lower-intermediate and above
Time:	60 minutes
Sites:	http://www.yahoo.com – Music -> Artists -> Beatles section

Procedure

Hand out the *Mind the gap* activity and give students time to complete what they can. Note that number eight has numerous possibilities (and no one correct answer), so see how many you can get from the group. Brainstorm information about The Beatles. What does the class know about them, and what would they like to know? Make a collaborative list of things to find.

There are a lot of Beatles sites in the Yahoo! section, so give students time to go through them and find the information they need. It would be a good idea to focus on the Yahoo! website summaries for categories, teaching students to look for relevant words such as 'discography' for the song titles and 'biography' for general information about the musicians. Students should check their answers to the *Mind the gap* activity and find the information they wanted to know.

Get feedback on the song titles and make sure the class has found the information needed. The information collected can then be built up into a small biography of The Beatles, or a Twenty Things You Didn't Know About The Beatles article.

Follow-on

Personalise the activity with more Internet time for students to find out a bit more about their favourite bands for a future writing project, including discography, biography, pictures, etc. For lower levels, this is an ideal opportunity for the celebrity interview practising the present tense, adverbs of frequency, etc. with students taking turns to play the part of a celebrity.

TIP ☑

More 'scholarly' information about the Beatles can be found at http://www.getback.org, which includes a Today in Beatles History section.

Mind the gap

These are all Beatles song titles. Can you complete them?

1 Lucy in the Sky with _____
2 Strawberry Fields _____
3 Can't Buy me _____
4 Do You Want to Know a _____
5 _____ Days a Week
6 Hello _____
7 Yellow _____
8 _____
9 She's _____ Home
10 Hard Day's _____

© Cambridge University Press 2007

2.19 Mystery postcards

Aim:	To write an imaginary holiday postcard
Focus:	Past tenses, present perfect tense, adjectives
Level:	Elementary and above
Time:	60 minutes
Sites:	http://www.hallmark.com

Procedure

Hand out a copy of the *Mystery postcard* and ask students where they think Graham and Cindy are on holiday. The answer should be Paris, France. How did they know? The clues are: Tower, boat on the river, art gallery, croissant, wine, Disney. Now ask them to think of somewhere they would like to go on holiday and to make a list of the things they would do and see there. This can also be done with somewhere they have already been.

Divide students into pairs. Go to the Hallmark site – Free E-Cards section – and give students time to prepare and send a mystery postcard to their partner. This involves choosing a card, writing the text for the card and addressing it (email address), previewing it to make sure it looks fine and then clicking *Send*.

Note that when a postcard is sent, notification is sent via email to the recipient who then has to return to the site to 'collect' the card. This is usually very quick, but you may need to continue this activity in a subsequent class if the cards don't arrive quickly enough. When the students have picked up their postcards, print them out.

Display the postcards in the classroom and give students time to walk around deciding where everyone is on holiday. They should make notes of the clues which helped them work out the answers. Get feedback and check everyone is right.

Follow-on
For higher levels, work on country stereotypes can be done, concentrating on adjectives and concepts used to describe people from different countries (e.g. English people all wear bowler hats and carry an umbrella and a copy of *The Times*. They are cold and a little arrogant ...). What is the purpose of stereotypes, and how much truth is there in them? For lower levels, a holiday diary is a fun follow-on.

Mystery postcard

Dear Mum and Dad,

It's really great here! The flight wasn't very long and we had good food on the plane.

It's a very expensive city, so we haven't been out too much. You were right, the view from the top of the Tower is amazing, you can see all of the city. Today we're going on a boat on the river and then to visit a couple of old churches before we go to that art gallery you told us about.

We've had lots of croissants and coffee for break-fast – very cheap! The wine is also good and cheap Disney at the weekend! Love, Graham and Cindy

Mr and Mrs Thomas

3 Blackberry Way

Gloucester

GR1 4XY

England

© Cambridge University Press 2007

2.20 A terrible holiday

Aim: To talk about holidays – good and bad
Focus: Past tenses, travel vocabulary
Level: Upper-intermediate and above
Time: 60 minutes
Sites: http://www.ivillage.co.uk/travel/community/essentials/articles/ 0,,598871_676057,00.html

Procedure
Brainstorm travel vocabulary in the following categories: getting there (transport and travelling), things to take (what to pack), where to stay (types of

holiday accommodation), what to do (holiday activities), people (hotel staff, tour guides, etc.). Build up a comprehensive list of vocabulary for students to use later. Hand out the *Best and worst* questionnaire and give students time to think and make notes before pairing them off to compare and discuss.

Have students look at the short holiday disaster stories at the iVillage site. Either prepare specific comprehension questions, or just get students to identify who is writing, what kind of holiday they were expecting, what went wrong and how the story ended. You might also initiate a discussion on which holiday was the most disastrous.

Using the structures and ideas from the website, students can now write up their own personal disaster holiday.

Follow-on

The disaster holiday articles could be displayed for review and comment. Students could also play the part of a travel company representative writing a letter of apology or explanation for the terrible holidays.

TIP ☑

There are just a few stories at this site, but they give a general idea of the kind of thing that can go wrong. If these are not enough for you, try Google for more disaster holidays.

Best and worst

Think about all the holidays you've had. Which one was the best, and which the worst? Make notes in the space below . . .

BEST	WORST
Reason	Reason ....
Where	Where ....
Who with	Who with ....
Weather	Weather ....
Food	Food ....
Company	Company ....
Activities	Activities ....

© Cambridge University Press 2007

2.21 A new logo

Aim:	To talk about logos, company philosophy and image
Focus:	Descriptions, making predictions
Level:	Mid-intermediate and above
Time:	60 minutes
Sites:	http://www.thelogofactory.com/

Procedure

Students bring examples of their company (or school) logo, letterheads and any other material which identifies the corporate image of the place where they work or study. They introduce their company/school and show how the features, services and philosophy of the company are reflected in the materials.

This page at The Logo Factory has a large collection of logos created for different companies by the design studio (click on the Logo Galleries link at the top of the page). Encourage students to look at the logos and predict what kind of company might have a logo like that. They should talk in groups and make predictions. Then allow them time to look at the descriptions of the logos which interest them by clicking on the logo and going to the corresponding page.

Bearing in mind what they have just seen, ask them to cast a more critical eye over their company/school image and discuss in groups what they think they might be able to do with it. If there are any artists (amateur or professional) in the class, ask them to help with the new designs.

Follow-on

Students could prepare a report for a design company, summarising their company/school image, philosophy and services and asking for a re-design of their logo, stationery, etc.

2.22 Written in the stars

Aim:	To talk about character / horoscopes
Focus:	Character adjectives, making predictions
Level:	Upper-intermediate and above
Time:	90 minutes
Sites:	http://www.astrology-online.com – horoscope section

Procedure

Do the *What are they like?* activity to do some basic work on the kind of character adjectives which usually occur in horoscopes. Does the class

71

believe in them? Do students read their horoscope every day? What star sign are they – and do they fit into the general description for that sign?

Give half the class six star signs, and the other half the remaining six. Give them time to visit the website and make some notes on the descriptions given to each sign (Sign Explanations section). At the top of each page there is a quick summary for the sign, so they don't have to go through the long descriptions which follow.

You should now have an information gap activity with students being able to get together in pairs and ask about the signs they didn't investigate. They can then chat about their personal horoscopes for the week. Do they think anything will come true (or has anything already come true)?

What are they like?

How would you describe someone who ...

gives away lots of money?	generous
never buys you a drink?	....
easily loses their temper?	....
never loses their temper?	....
helps other people?	....
only thinks about themselves?	....
jokes about everything?	....
never jokes about anything?	....
expects good things to happen?	....
expects bad things to happen?	....
believes whatever you tell them?	....
doubts what you tell them?	....
worries about what people think?	....
doesn't care what people think?	....
likes going to parties?	....
doesn't like going to parties?	....
lets people down?	....
never lets people down?	....
has a high opinion of themselves?	....
doesn't boast?	....

© Cambridge University Press 2007

Follow-on

A good follow-on is a 'Find someone who . . .' activity with a walkround in class (e.g. 'Find someone who . . . thinks they are a typical Aries', 'Find someone who . . . doesn't agree with the description of their personality on the website', etc.). Higher levels can have a more in-depth discussion about prediction, astrology, etc.

Another follow-on might be to let them visit the page with their horoscope for the week (Weekly Horoscope section) and make some notes on what they can expect, then compare in small groups. You can follow up on this in a later class: did any of it come true?

2.23 People watching

Aim:	To describe people
Focus:	Adjectives, activities, present continuous tense
Level:	Elementary and above
Time:	60 minutes
Sites:	http://www.onlinephotogallery.com/people.htm

Procedure

This activity requires some pre-Internet work on descriptions: physical characteristics, clothing, location and activity. I have often used the Suzanne Vega song 'Tom's Diner' as a scene-setting device since it features descriptions of people in a café and is easily exploitable for the present continuous tense. The song itself can be done as a gap-fill with the participles removed, and students can be invited to imagine or even illustrate the scene they hear in the song (remember, you can find the lyrics on the Net – see *Activity 2.5 A song class*).

The gallery of photos in the website is a selection of thumbnail images (small versions of larger ones) which can be clicked and enlarged. Give students time to look around and decide on one photo they find particularly interesting. They should then imagine who the person is, where they live and what they are like, what they do (job and hobbies) and what their life is like. They should rough out a quick description of the person. These can be stuck to the wall, and the class can read them and try to identify the person on screen.

With the details they have got from the photo, and their notes, a longer description can now be worked on, with students extending the short notes they made to a full-blown description of the person and their life.

Follow-on

Very low levels can use this activity on one particular basis, concentrating simply on clothes, or physical description, or activity.

With more creative classes, try incorporating the characters chosen and described into a song (following the example of 'Tom's Diner'), or a simple poem.

With higher levels, some useful work can be done on stereotyping. What assumptions underlay their guesses, and were they fair assumptions? For example, a fair assumption might be that a blond-haired person is likely to be from Northern Europe, whereas an ungrounded prejudice might be that someone with glasses is probably an intellectual, etc.

TIP ☑

Also try searching for 'pictures of people' on Google. There are a lot of image archives on the Net. These usually contain copyright material, so you can look at them on-screen, but there are usually rules about saving them onto your own computer. Check before you do.

2.24 Get a job

Aim:	To find the right job / talk about skills and character
Focus:	Personality adjectives, occupations, describing daily routine
Level:	Upper-intermediate and above
Time:	60 minutes
Sites:	http://www.queendom.com/tests/personality/type_a_r_access.html
	http://quiz.ivillage.co.uk/uk_work/tests/career.htm

Procedure

Use a copy of a jobs page from an English language newspaper for an introductory speed reading activity with general comprehension questions such as: which company wants dynamic young managers? Where will you get two months' paid holiday per year? (If you don't have access to a newspaper, try one of the jobs pages on the Net.) Now elicit a selection of popular jobs and discuss what skills and personal qualities are necessary for each one.

Start with the Queendom personality quiz – once done, students can find out which jobs suit their personality. If you have already done work on character, go directly to the 'What career will suit your personality?' quiz. Give students a chance to work through the material and come up with a selection of jobs they think may suit them.

Use the *Ideal job* activity with younger students. This will need adapting for adults who are already working. You could concentrate on the jobs they are doing now and the ones recommended on the website. What would they do if they could choose any job?

Follow-on

Play a game with students asking questions to establish the occupation of one member of the class. Questions can only be answered with 'yes' or 'no'. This can also be done using mime with the student doing a short visual representation of their job before taking questions.

Alternatively use a selection of job pictures, letting a student decide on one and describe the qualities needed to do the job. The rest of the class has to guess which job picture is being described. This is also an ideal opportunity to do language work on daily routine.

TIP ☑

The personality quiz can be done as a starter. If students already know what kind of personality they have, they can go straight to the 'What career will suit your personality?' section. A 'kid-friendly' version of this activity can be done here: http://www.kidzworld.com/site/p2815.htm

---

Ideal job

Think about the questions below and make some notes:

- What jobs do you think you would like to do?
- What qualities are needed for them?
- What did you find out on the iVillage website
  - about your personality?
  - about recommended jobs?
- Have you changed your mind after using the iVilllage?
- Which of the recommended jobs interests you most?
- What do you think a typical day in this job would be like?

© Cambridge University Press 2007

2.25 Cooking with kids

Aim:	To look at recipes for young people
Focus:	Food vocabulary, describing processes, likes and dislikes
Level:	Elementary and above (young learners)
Time:	60 minutes
Sites:	http://www.kidchef.com/cda/recipes.cfm

Procedure

Food and drink vocabulary is one of the areas which young learners usually cover in depth. Take time out now to do some revision of fruit, vegetables, drinks, etc. Brainstorm the vocabulary onto the board in various categories. Do the *Some of my favourite things* activity. This is also an opportunity to do some work on expressing likes and dislikes. Get some feedback as a class, and make a top ten food and drink chart based on their preferences.

There are lots of recipes for kids on the Kid Chef site, divided into various categories. Some of them have fun names and are often very colourful and easy to make. Make a questionnaire, e.g. What fruits are on the Fruit Pizza? What's in a Witches Brew? Be careful to choose easy recipes and questions.

Get feedback on the questionnaire and clear up any problems which have arisen. Now have a competition to design the most exotic sandwich, or the strangest drink. Encourage students to write a description of how to make the food or drink, to draw an illustration and to think of a fun name for it.

Follow-on

If you're truly adventurous and have the facilities, you could try producing some of the recipes in class – or maybe have a Fun Food competition with everyone making something at home and bringing it into class for a party.

TIP ☑

These recipes use American English vocabulary, so if you are teaching in a British (or other) English context, you may have to do some work on the vocabulary differences (see *Activity 2.16 The same language?*).

Some of my favourite things

Complete the sentences about food and drink.

My favourite drink is . . . .

My favourite food is . . . .

I love . . . .

I hate . . . .

I never eat . . . .

For breakfast I usually have . . . .

I usually have lunch at . . . .

My perfect dinner is . . . .

Now ask your partner questions about food and drink.

2.26 Playing it safe

Aim: To find out about Internet security
Focus: Imperatives, advice
Level: Elementary and above
Time: 60 minutes
Sites: http://www.worldkids.net/school/safety/internet

Procedure

Start with a general discussion of computer usage, perhaps using the *TechnoKids* activity. Find out as a class who has a computer and what they use it for. Who plays games, and what kinds of games do they play? Who has access to the Internet at home, and what do they use it for? You could also try eliciting what some of the dangers or problems with using the Internet might be before going online.

Give students time to look through the safety tips and make notes to summarise them later. You might want to set a small comprehension task to go with the reading.

Discuss the safety tips put forward. Which are the most important ones, and which ones do they think are unimportant? Are there any they don't understand? Is there any information they think should be added?

Draw up a set of rules for Internet use in the classroom. Negotiate with the class. This can become a useful contract for general computer use behaviour during the course.

TIP ☑

The Internet has plenty of questionable material, and – as in real life – has users who are all-too-willing to take advantage of young people. This is a valuable lesson for young people on the dos and don'ts of Internet life. Note that the *TechnoKids* activity is similar to the questionnaire in *Activity 2.1 Introduction to the Net (I)* – choose the version that best suits your learners.

TechnoKids

Talking about computers:

- Have you got a computer at home?
  - What do you use it for?
  - Do you play computer games? (what kinds of games?)
  - Do you use it for homework? (how do you use it?)
- Have you got Internet access at home?
  - What do you use it for?
  - Do you use email? (who do you write to?)
  - Do you look at webpages? (what kinds of webpages?)
- Do you think you use your computer too much?

© Cambridge University Press 2007

2.27 Olympic Games

Aim:	To find out about the Olympic Games
Focus:	Sports vocabulary, mixed tenses (past)
Level:	Mid-intermediate and above
Time:	60 minutes
Sites:	http://www.aafla.org/6oic/primer_frmst.htm

Procedure

If the Games have ever been held in the country / city where you teach, you have an ideal opportunity to introduce the topic. What happened during the games? Were they good or bad for the country / city? How did the image of the country / city change after the Games? If this is not the case, simply move straight into eliciting information about the Games. What does the class know about them, and what would they like to know?

Using the *Just a game* activity, visit the Olympic Primer site and give students a chance to answer the questions as well as to look for the information already discussed in class.

Get feedback on the questionnaire. Were they surprised by anything they read? Imagine that the Games are going to be held in their city (assuming that they haven't already!). What improvements would they have to make? Plan what should be done, and design a logo and mascot for the games. This could also be turned into an extended project as suggested below.

Follow-on
An interesting follow-on is to design a bid for the city you live in. Why should the Games come there? This could be built up into a web-based project. (See *Section 3* for ideas.)

Just a game

What do you know about the Olympic Games?

Where and when did the Games start?
How often do they take place?
Who revived the Olympic Games, and when?
Where are the Games being held next?
Where is the International Olympic Committee based?
What is the Olympic symbol, and what does it signify?
Can you name three Olympic mascots?
Which country first televised the Olympics? In which year?
What is doping?
Why were the 1936 Games controversial?

© Cambridge University Press 2007

2.28 The London sightseeing tour

Aim: To plan a day out in London
Focus: Making arrangements, suggesting, agreeing, disagreeing
Level: Lower-intermediate and above
Time: 60 minutes
Sites: http://www.londontown.com

Procedure
Start off with a general chat about London. Have any of the students visited the city? What did they do there? What did they visit and see? Get students

into groups of three and four and give them time to talk to each other and find out what they like doing when they visit a new city. Do they like seeing monuments, going shopping, visiting galleries, etc.? Now tell them they are going to plan a day out in London, between them, and that they must try to agree on what to see and do and to accommodate the likes and dislikes of each member of the group.

The London Town website has complete coverage of things to see and do in London. Steer students towards sections such as Attractions, Sightseeing, Events and Travel. There are also sections on restaurants, shopping, etc.

Once they have agreed, have them complete the *London sightseeing tour* worksheet. Re-distribute the group members to make new groups with everyone explaining to the others what their group decided to do, where to go, etc. If you have paper maps of the city or other realia, these can make the activity more interesting. For those with unlimited Internet time, stay with the computers for a more interesting description, using the website.

Follow-on

A logical follow-on is to design a similar resource for the city your students live in. Decide on the major features of the city. Why would someone want to visit it, and what should they do while there? What other information would they need to know to have a successful visit?

TIP ☑

Most major world cities have plenty of websites devoted to them. Look in Yahoo! or google for a city which suits you and your students best. This activity also works well in a Business English class.

London sightseeing tour

Write a brief summary of times and activities as you plan them.

TIME		ACTIVITY
8 am	–	breakfast in the hotel
....	–	....
....	–	....
....	–	....
....	–	....
....	–	....

© Cambridge University Press 2007

2.29 What's the time?

Aim:	To talk about the time around the world
Focus:	The time
Level:	Elementary and above (young learners)
Time:	40 minutes
Sites:	http://www.timeanddate.com/worldclock/

Procedure

This works well as a revision activity for telling the time – something which is done in almost all beginner courses, but often still not mastered properly even after three or four years of study. Make sure you do some pre-teaching or reminding before visiting the website.

Distribute the *What's the time?* activity and give students time on the website to answer the questions. Bear in mind that most of the times noted from the website will only vary by a few minutes, so this activity alone will not practise the full range of times you might want to cover.

In pairs, students ask and answer from the *What's the time?* activity. Move on to a more personalised activity with students talking to each other about their daily routines, e.g. What time do you get up? This can then be turned into a writing activity, 'A Day in the Life of …'.

What's the time?

Find out the time in these places.   **Find out the time in these places.**

STUDENT A   **STUDENT B**

Amsterdam . . . .   Ottawa . . . .
Taipei . . . .   Sydney . . . .
Stockholm . . . .   San Francisco . . . .
Rome . . . .   Rio de Janeiro . . . .
New York . . . .   Moscow . . . .
Mexico City . . . .   Hong Kong . . . .

Now ask your partner about …   **Now ask your partner about …**
Ottawa . . . .   Amsterdam . . . .
Sydney . . . .   Taipei . . . .
San Francisco . . . .   Stockholm . . . .
Rio de Janeiro . . . .   Rome . . . .
Moscow . . . .   New York . . . .
Hong Kong . . . .   Mexico City . . . .

© Cambridge University Press 2007

Variation

You can also do some work on nationalities and countries using the webpage. A slightly more complex activity would be to quiz students by country, rather than by city. They would then have to use their search skills to find out which cities on the time page are from which country, before being able to answer the time questions. To get a full range of times to practise, visit a TV company page and make a similar activity with the TV listings page, basing the questions around the formula: What time is the news on TVE1?, etc.

2.30 Dream holiday

Aim:	To plan the perfect holiday
Focus:	Talking about holidays and travel plans
Level:	Upper-intermediate and above
Time:	60 minutes
Sites:	http://www.lonelyplanet.com

Procedure

Start off with a simple questionnaire on holiday preferences. Get feedback as a class and give students the opportunity to talk to anyone who may have been to a country they would like to visit themselves.

Tell the class that money is no object and that they can go where they want and travel how they want. They have one month of holiday to organise. They must decide where they are going to go, how they are going to travel, what they'll do when they get there, etc.

Students form small groups and tell each other about their dream holiday. They can also inform their colleagues about the climate, geography, food and culture of their chosen destination(s).

Follow-on

This activity can be extended further with more detailed planning of the travel arrangements including looking for airline tickets and finding out train and coach details – all of which is easily accomplished on the Net. A good place to start is the Yahoo! Travel section.

Dream holiday

**Think about these questions, then get into groups and discuss them.
What would your dream holiday be like?**

- Where would you like to go?
- What would you do?
- Who would you go with?
- How would you travel?

© Cambridge University Press 2007

2.31 A night at the movies

Aim:	To plan a night out at the movies
Focus:	Likes and dislikes, cinema vocabulary, arranging to go out
Level:	Mid-intermediate and above
Time:	60 minutes
Sites:	http://www.bbc.co.uk/movies/

Procedure

The *Movie crossword* is a good starting point for this activity, as it activates
a lot of the vocabulary which will be needed in the following parts. Students
should walk around finding out who likes which types of films, and getting
together into like-minded groups before going online.

The BBC Movies section has reviews of forthcoming and recent releases.
Give students time to see which films are on at the cinema, and to decide
which one they would like to see. Encourage negotiation during this part.
Further investigation can be done online to find out where the films are on
and to arrange which cinema to go to, and at what time.

Get feedback as a group, exchanging experiences and decisions. I usually
like to follow this activity up with a look at the 100 Greatest Films website.
This can easily be turned into an information gap activity if printed out.
Take the top twenty films and make two copies of the lists, then blank out
the titles – or partial titles – of half the films on each copy. Students then see
which titles they can complete (or guess) and ask their partner questions to
fill the gaps on their copy.

You can also use this site as a springboard for students to make a personal
(or class) list of their top ten films of all time. They might start by deleting all
the ones they have never heard of, then get into groups to strike off any of the

remaining ones they think are not very good before finally choosing ten from the remaining titles.

Movie crossword

ACROSS

1 Animated films (8)
4 A type of film involving a journey (4, 5)
6 Famous kung fu actor (5, 3)
11 Film award (5)
13 You need to buy this to see a film (6)
14 You make a film with a ... (6)
16 Do you want to go ... the cinema? (2)
17 What's on ... the cinema tonight? (2)
18 Film with cowboys and Indians (7)
19 Are there any good films ... tonight? (2)
21 An exciting kind of film (8)
22 Text on screen in a foreign film (8)
23 Explosions, fights, battles ... (7,7)

DOWN

2 Male performer in a film (5)
3 Where most science fiction films are set (5)
4 Round metal container for film (4)
5 Filmed ... in Africa (2,8)
6 Old films were made in ... (5,3,5)
7 Frightening type of film (6)
8 You eat this in the cinema (7)
9 Famous film alien (1,1)
10 Short advert for a film (7)
12 A funny film (6)
15 *Alien* was set on a ... (9)
16 There's one ... woman in the film. It's definitely a very male story (5)
20 The story of a film (4)

© Cambridge University Press 2007

KEY: Across – 1 cartoons, 4 road movie, 6 Bruce Lee, 11 Oscar, 13 ticket, 14 camera, 16 to, 17 at, 18 western, 19 on, 21 thriller, 22 subtitle, 23 special effects

Down – 2 actor, 3 space, 4 reel, 5 on location, 6 black and white, 7 horror, 8 popcorn, 9 ET, 10 trailer, 12 comedy, 15 spaceship, 16 token, 20 plot

Follow-on
Film titles are often wildly changed when they are translated into other languages. *The Sound of Music*, for example, was called *Sonrisas y Lágrimas* in Spain (this translates as *Smiles and Tears*). A good activity is a matching exercise with original titles and the titles from the country where you are teaching.

A written assignment of a film review is another good activity to round off this cinema class.

TIP ☑

A good site for movie reviews is http://www.filmsite.org/momentsindx.html These sites (like me!) use 'movie' and 'film' interchangeably – make sure your students are aware of this practice.

2.32 Classified ads

Aim: To investigate online shopping
Focus: Describing things
Level: Advanced
Time: 60 minutes
Sites: http://www.loot.com

Procedure
Start off with the **Birthday shopping** questionnaire, individually, then in pairs. Then get feedback as a group. Now tell students they have a certain amount of money to buy presents for their family and that they are going to do their shopping online.

Loot has an extremely efficient search facility, so it will be easy for students to find what they are looking for this way. Alternatively, they can browse one of the sections until they find what they are looking for (e.g. Travel, Music, Electrical). The idea here is to fill up their shopping list within budget.

Get students into groups to explain what they have bought (virtually, rather than actually!), how much they paid for each item and who it is for. They should try to explain why they think each item is suitable for the person they are going to give it to.

Follow-on

A good follow-on is to organise an unwanted gift swap. Give out two or three pictures of gifts to each student and explain they got them for their birthday (or similar occasion) and now they don't want them (old catalogues or magazines are a good source of useful pictures for this type of activity). Have them write up small ads for each of the products, with descriptions and prices and then organise a walkround market, with students bartering with each other to exchange what they have for things they really want.

TIP ☑

Another good classifieds site is: http://www.nettrader.co.uk
Classified adverts use a lot of shorthand and abbreviations, so you may want to do some work on these before visiting the site.

Birthday shopping

Think about these questions and make some notes.

What do you usually get for your birthday?
What would you like to get for your birthday?
Do you enjoy shopping for presents for other people?
Do you enjoy buying things for yourself?

Who do you usually buy presents for?
What did you buy them last time?
If you could buy them anything, what would you buy?

Write the names of the people you usually buy presents for and then make a list of what you would buy them if you could.

© Cambridge University Press 2007

2.33 Finding a flat

Aim:	To shop for a new home online
Focus:	Describing houses and homes
Level:	Upper-intermediate and above
Time:	60 minutes
Sites:	http://www.findaproperty.com/coun0001.html

Procedure

Get students talking about where they live and what they think makes a good home. Get feedback as a group. Each student should imagine they are going to London, some to study, some to work in low-paid jobs, some in well-paid jobs. Each of them should be told how much money they have, what they are going to be doing, where they will be working or studying and whether they should be looking for a rental or to buy somewhere.

The students' task is to find a suitable property either to rent or to buy. They must try to find something in the area where they are going to work.

Get students in small groups to tell each other what they have found and to describe their new homes.

Follow-on

Get students to write a letter from their new home, describing it and the surrounding area to friends or family. This provides good practice of all the vocabulary encountered during the actual activity. For lower levels, you could use the online estate agents offices to practise furniture vocabulary as well as *it has got,* there is and *there are.*

TIP ☑

Also worth trying are Bushells at http://www.bushells.com which has photos to go with the adverts and http://www.net-lettings.co.uk/ which deals more with rentals. These sites also deal with commercial properties, so can be used in a business English context.

2.34 Suits you

Aim:	To talk about clothing and fashion
Focus:	Vocabulary connected with clothing and fashion
Level:	Elementary and above
Time:	60 minutes
Sites:	http://www.frenchconnection.co.uk/collection_06ss.html www.riverisland.com

Procedure

With lower levels, you'll need to pre-teach the clothing vocabulary you intend to focus on. With higher levels, start with the *Fashion* speaking activity. Make sure all the vocabulary you'll need for the activity comes out in this part of the class.

Included here are two examples of online clothes shops – you can choose the male or female section and look round their collections. Lower levels can use the pictures as visual cues for descriptions which can be oral or written up later. Higher levels should 'go shopping' for new clothes – a virtual shopping trip, with students finding clothes they like the look of and inviting opinion from the others, just as in a real shopping trip.

Fashion

Are you worried about fashion and trends?

- What's your favourite outfit for work / school?
- What about at the weekend?
- What do you wear when you go out socially?
- What do you wear around the house?
- Which of these things would you wear, and which wouldn't you wear?

Flared jeans	A checked shirt	A fur coat
A waistcoat (vest)	A flowery shirt	A three-piece suit
High-heeled shoes	A hoodie	Striped trousers
A baseball cap	Cowboy boots	A mini-skirt
A denim jacket	Torn jeans	A woolly hat
Stockings	A sweatshirt	A cardigan

© Cambridge University Press 2007

Variation
An alternative start activity is to have students do a walkround of some kind
(e.g. a 'Find someone who . . .' activity) then put them in pairs back-to-back
and have them describe what the other is wearing.

Follow-on
As a follow-on, with lower levels and young learners, cut-out items of
clothing (or student drawings) can be used to dress sketches of people and
then describe them: 'Susan is wearing . . .'.

Teenagers can organise a fashion show, with people taking it in turns to
announce who is on the catwalk and what they are wearing, describing
everything as if it's the latest fashion. It's a good idea for the teacher to have
the first go, just to break the ice!

2.35 A fine day out

Aim:	To get travel information
Focus:	Times and timetables / travel information
Level:	Mid-intermediate and above
Time:	60 minutes
Sites:	http://www.traveline.org.uk/index.htm

Procedure
This is an ideal opportunity to do some work on travel vocabulary, so do the
Travel tips activity as a warm-up. At lower levels, concentrate on the
prepositions (by train, on foot, etc.). With higher levels, focus on the
problem area of trip, excursion, voyage, journey, etc.

Give out a set of tasks concerning finding train times, plane times, prices,
etc. Students should be given questions such as, *How much is a return ticket
from London to Edinburgh? What time does the first coach to Bristol leave?
Is it cheaper to fly or get the train from London to Edinburgh?* This is best
done as an 'interactive reading race' in teams. You write out the questions on
separate slips of paper and place them on your desk. Students take a
question and look for the answer before returning it and taking another. This
process is repeated until all the questions have been answered.

If you don't like the idea of making this kind of exercise too competitive,
simply introduce a time limit to the activity, with students finding as many
answers as possible within the given time frame.

Variation
This can be set up as a typical travel agent scenario with some students having
the tasks and other students being travel agents using the Net to get the

information. As the travel agents will be very busy, encourage the customers to make small talk as they sit waiting for the answers – just like in real life!

TIP ☑

The Traveline site has links to all major travel organisations in the UK, including airlines, train companies, coach and bus companies, etc. Some of these services (for example The Train Line, which allows online booking of train tickets) require you to register before using them – registration is free, but it's a good idea to do it before the class. Again, this activity is easily adapted to other countries, using the Yahoo! Travel section as a starting point for finding resources.

Travel tips

How do you like to travel?
How do you usually travel during the week?
And at the weekend?
Do you prefer a car or bicycle to public transport? Why?
How do you travel when you go on holiday?
What's the longest flight you've ever been on?
What about the longest boat trip / train or coach journey?

Now get into small groups and compare your answers.

© Cambridge University Press 2007

2.36 But is it art?

Aim:	To talk about art
Focus:	Describing things, giving opinions, biographies
Level:	Upper-intermediate and above
Time:	60 minutes
Sites:	http://www.artsearch.net

Procedure

You need a set of postcards or colour photocopies of famous paintings by famous people. You might even like to invite each student to bring in a postcard or magazine cut-out showing a painting. Give students a chance to walk around examining them, but don't let them see any details yet – just the picture. Get students into pairs and ask each pair to choose a picture they particularly like. Pre-teach some vocabulary for describing pictures (e.g. 'in the foreground', 'in the background', 'on the horizon', etc.).

Starting at the Art Search page, ask students to find out some information about the picture they have chosen, and the artist who painted it. They should get biographical information, history of the picture and details of other work done by the artist.

Each of the pairs is now in charge of a special exhibition in the class. Their job is to give a small introduction to the exhibition, talking about their chosen painting and giving some background information on the artist.

Variation
A simple alternative introduction to the task involves dividing the class into pairs and giving each member of the pair a simple sketch to describe to their partner, who has to draw it.

Follow-on
As a follow-on, a written description of one of the postcards is a good activity.

2.37 Puzzlemaker

Aim:	To make and solve puzzles
Focus:	Vocabulary revision
Level:	Elementary and above (young learners)
Time:	60 minutes
Sites:	http://www.puzzlemaker.com

Procedure
There are lots of different ways of using Puzzlemaker, but I think my favourite is as a regular vocabulary revision activity. This is an idea for using the wordsearch maker. Get students in pairs to brainstorm vocabulary for a particular area you have been working on recently (or not so recently), e.g. food and drink, travel or similar. Have them make a list of 15–20 words they can remember from the field.

Show students how to use the wordsearch maker. All they then have to do is fill in the form and have the webpage make their wordsearch for them. Encourage them to personalise the title. Make sure you print a copy of each quiz when it is finished.

Photocopy the quizzes and distribute them over the following classes, either as quick activities in class or for homework. I like to use this regularly as it gives the students some investment in the work done in class, and there's the added challenge of being able to make a puzzle which can't be solved by their colleagues.

Follow-on

Investigate the other types of puzzles – most of them are easy to make, and once your students have learnt each type they will be able to make them unsupervised.

Gavin's Fruit Wordsearch

```
G  T  T  C  F  J  R  A  U  C  D  K  E  V  S
O  L  I  R  P  Y  O  E  Q  I  H  F  E  E  N
R  K  J  U  M  B  U  Q  P  A  Z  E  X  J  K
A  F  L  L  R  J  Z  K  Y  E  X  N  R  I  P
N  B  V  A  L  F  A  T  N  P  F  I  H  R  H
G  O  E  G  A  A  E  I  C  A  S  R  A  O  Y
E  T  Z  N  V  D  R  P  M  R  U  E  Z  L  P
J  M  F  Q  U  A  Q  W  A  G  P  G  W  T  I
X  Q  V  E  D  R  N  U  O  R  H  N  I  F  B
V  W  B  N  I  Y  P  Y  U  L  G  A  U  C  O
Q  Z  A  O  A  N  O  L  E  M  P  T  U  F  E
Z  M  B  P  F  X  U  Y  V  G  E  M  L  G  B
N  N  P  K  S  S  S  Z  Z  F  S  U  I  Z  X
V  L  P  I  W  L  O  J  B  A  N  A  N  A  G
```

PRUNE	ORANGE	MANDARIN	PEAR
GRAPE	BANANA	TANGERINE	
MELON	GRAPEFRUIT	CHERRY	

2.38 Holiday posters

Aim:	To make posters for celebrations
Focus:	Image searching
Level:	Elementary and above (young learners)
Time:	60 minutes
Sites:	http://www.kidsdomain.com/clip/

Procedure

Have a look at some good posters in class. What do students think makes a good poster? Then get students to do a rough sketch of what they would like to put on their posters.

Use one of the clipart galleries to find suitable pictures for the posters. Make sure you save any useful pictures by right-clicking on them and choosing the *Save Picture As ...* option (and remember where you save them!).

Work with the students to produce their posters using a word processor such as Microsoft Word and the pictures they have saved from the Net. For very young learners, Microsoft produce a word processor called Creative Writer which can be used easily to make posters, invitations, cards, etc. This idea can be used to coincide with major festivals such as Christmas, Easter or local celebrations in your city or country.

Variation

Adapt this activity to higher levels, with posters for pop concerts, theatre events, etc. Business English classes can work on new advertising campaigns for their companies, or logo designs.

TIP ☑

Google and Yahoo! both have excellent images searches. There are also plenty of clipart collections on the Net, and you can find themed sets of pictures for most areas of life (try searching in Google for 'free clipart' or 'clipart collection'). Also try xtock.xchng at http://www.sxc.hu/ and http://yahooligans.yahoo.com/
Please make sure that you are free to use the pictures you find on the Net.

2.39 Nice day today

Aim:	To talk about the weather
Focus:	Weather vocabulary and structures
Level:	Elementary and above
Time:	60 minutes
Sites:	http://weather.yahoo.com
Notes:	See also *Activity 2.9 The weather*

Procedure

The Yahoo! weather site uses the standard symbols for rain, cloud, storm, etc. Print these out (or draw your own) and use them to pre-teach or revise ways of talking about the weather (don't forget to do work on 'it's rainy' and 'it's raining', etc.).

This is a simple ask and answer activity with students looking for details of the weather in various places (around the world) and then asking their partner about other places. Give them time to find the places and make notes before leaving the computers. Students complete the *Weather forecast* activity by asking and answering.

Follow-on

A world map can make a nice addition to this activity, especially for younger learners. As they ask and answer about the weather, they can draw the appropriate symbols on the weather map. This is also a good opportunity to do some work on country names.

For higher levels, use the long-range forecast from the Yahoo! page for the country where you live and have students pretend to be weather forecasters on the TV. If you can, put a sketch of the country on the board and get them to stick weather symbols on it as they deliver the forecast.

Weather forecast

Find out what the weather is like in …

STUDENT A	STUDENT B
London	Rome
Mexico City	Reykjavik
Sydney	Buenos Aires
New York	Moscow
Cairo	Toronto
Berlin	Tokyo

Now ask your partner about …

Rome	London
Reykjavik	Mexico City
Buenos Aires	Sydney
Moscow	New York
Toronto	Cairo
Tokyo	Berlin

© Cambridge University Press 2007

2.40 Disaster area

Aim:	To talk about world problems
Focus:	Global issues
Level:	Advanced
Time:	60 minutes
Sites:	http://dir.yahoo.com/Society_and_Culture/Issues_and_Causes/

Procedure

Give each student time to complete the *Disaster area* activity, then make
pairs and have them negotiate a new order and compare their answers to the
last two points. Gradually combine the groups until the whole class has
decided on a final order for the problems. Divide the class into four groups
and distribute the top four problems, one to each group.

The idea here is for each group to get as much information as possible about
the theme they have been given: the size and importance of the problem,
principal countries affected, the global implications of the problem, etc.

Students should do a presentation of the material they have found. When
all the presentations have been done, a vote should be taken on which cause
to support. Students can then use the Internet for further investigation into
how to do something to help. For example, the Hunger Page at
www.thehungersite.com donates money for food to starving countries every
time a link is clicked from their site. This is financed by large institutions and
could become a daily visit for your class.

Follow-on

This whole activity would make an ideal vehicle for an extended web
project. (See *Section 3*.)

Disaster area

**Here are various problems the world faces. Put them in order according
to how important you think they are.**

☐ Famine   ☐ Destruction of the ozone layer
☐ Poverty   ☐ Greenhouse Effect
☐ Over-population   ☐ Pollution
☐ Destruction of forests   ☐ Expansion of deserts
☐ War   ☐ Disease

Can you add any more to the list?

Do you think any of them are related to each other?

© Cambridge University Press 2007

2.41 Kids and the news

Aim: To explore current events with younger learners
Focus: General language
Level: Lower-intermediate and above (young learners)
Time: 60 minutes
Sites: http://yahooligans.yahoo.com/content/news/

Procedure

Print out five or six photos from the Yahoo! site, finding ones which are suitable for your class and level. Organise a guessing activity where students have to guess what each news story is, and write down three words connected with each story. This activity can easily be adapted for the Net, making it a more interactive activity.

Give students a chance to look around the site, find the photographs and see for themselves what stories were represented by the pictures. They should also check if the words they thought of are in each story.

Brainstorm some interesting or unusual events that have happened locally, then divide the class into groups and assign one event to each. They should then find a suitable photograph on the web, and write a short paragraph to illustrate their story.

Follow-on

As a follow-on, print the stories and have the students illustrate them, either with their own drawings, or with pictures from magazines and newspapers. Then organise an exhibition of the work.

2.42 It's a mystery

Aim: To learn about secret codes
Focus: Numbers, the alphabet
Level: Elementary and above
Time: 60 minutes
Sites: http://russells.freeshell.org/enigma/

Procedure

You'll need to pre-teach the numbers 1–26 and the letters of the alphabet or do some revision of them if your students are already familiar with them. I like to do alphabet races round the class to revise the alphabet quickly, and games such as bingo are excellent for number revision.

Write the letters of the alphabet on the board, then write the numbers underneath, '1' below 'A', '2' below 'B', etc. Write a simple sentence on the board using numbers (something like My name is Gavin, which would be 13 25 14 1 13 5 9 19 7 1 22 9 13) and get students to tell you the correct letter for each number until they have discovered the message. Now do the *Secret messages* activity, with student A dictating their numbers and Student B writing in the number and saying the corresponding letter until they discover the words. You may need to change the words I have used to suit your group.

Russell's site features a working model of the Enigma Machine – a code maker and breaker from the Second World War. Give students a chance to set their code and encode a short message to someone else in the class before passing on the message and the key. Recipients of a coded message should set the machine up and decode the message.

Follow-on
Students can be invited to invent their own codes. Show them how to invert the numbers so that the alphabet-number code is also inverted, or to skip a number so that A becomes 1, B becomes 3, etc. Once they have invented a code, other students can have fun trying to break it.

TIP ☑

http://www.quizland.com/hiero.htm will convert names and short phrases written normally into their hieroglyphic equivalents. Ask students if they like how their name looks in ancient hieroglyphics and invite them to improve on it by drawing their own symbols to represent their name. For more code fun, try http://www.decodersite.com/

Secret messages

Student A
Birthday (2 9 _ _ _ _ _ _)
(_ _ _ _ _ _) . . . .
Bedroom (_ _ _ _ _ _ _)
(_ _ _ _ _ _ _ _ _) . . . .
Sandwich (_ _ _ _ _ _ _ _)
(_ _ _ _ _ _) . . . .
Football (_ _ _ _ _ _ _ _)
(_ _ _ _ _ _ _) . . . .

Student B
(_ _ _ _ _ _ _ _) . . . .
School (19 3 _ _ _ _)
(_ _ _ _ _ _ _) . . . .
Television (_ _ _ _ _ _ _ _ _ _)
(_ _ _ _ _ _ _ _) . . . .
Bicycle (_ _ _ _ _ _ _)
(_ _ _ _ _ _ _ _) . . . .
Armchair (_ _ _ _ _ _ _ _)

© Cambridge University Press 2007

2.43 Australian wildlife

Aim:	To find out about animal life in Australia
Focus:	Facts and figures, colours, habits
Level:	Elementary and above
Time:	60 minutes
Sites:	http://www.worldkids.net/critters/marsupials/

Procedure

Start by eliciting some information about Australia. This could be anything from soap operas such as *Neighbours*, to the Olympic Games. If the subject of animal life doesn't come out, introduce the theme. Do students know any Australian animals? If so, get some information on the board.

There are plenty of pages on the Marsupial Museum page, each one dealing with a different animal (note that not all marsupials come from Australia). Each page has at least one picture and some information about the animal. The language is not overly difficult here, but you will need to be prepared for some problems. A controlled reading task is the best way of approaching this. The *Animal facts* worksheet is designed for this. Give pairs of students one animal to investigate. Younger students can also be encouraged to draw the animal they see on the page, or colour in a picture of it.

Use the information you have gathered to make an Australian Animals Gallery, with students illustrating the *Animal facts* worksheet with a picture of the animal in question.

Variation

As a preliminary activity for the website, try printing out pictures of the animals you want to study, and having students label the pictures with the names of the animals.

Follow-on

A follow-on project could be done on the animal life in the country where you teach; this could even become a web project. Another quick follow-on activity is to make a wordsearch with the animal names. (See *Activity 2.37 Puzzlemaker.*)

TIP ☑

More can be found at http://www.kipandco.com.au/Main/Wildlife/wildlife.html and http://www.abc.net.au/nature/links/default.htm

---

Animal facts

Fill in the grid with the information you find:

Name of animal	
Colour	
Size	
Food	
Habits	

© Cambridge University Press 2007

2.44 Theme park

Aim: To design a theme park
Focus: Descriptions, agreeing and disagreeing, making suggestions
Level: Mid-intermediate and above
Time: 60 minutes
Sites: http://dlpfan.org/int/s7007.htm http://www.disney.com

Procedure

A general class discussion on theme parks and days out is a good start. What can you do if you want a day out where you live? Has anyone been to Disneyland? What kinds of rides or other activities do people like?

There are five principal parts to the Disneyland website (Mainstreet USA, Frontierland, Adventureland, Fantasyland, Discoveryland) modelled on the original in America. Divide the class into five groups and give them one part each. Give them time to look around their part of the park and decide what they would like to do there. Ask them to make notes on the different activities.

Redistribute the students into different groups, ensuring that each group has at least one member from each of the original five groups. Now tell them that they have won a weekend away at Disneyland and that they have to organise what they are going to do. When they have mapped out their two-day stay at the theme park, they give other groups a rundown of what they would do. Encourage comment and discussion on the best way to spend the two days.

Follow-on

An excellent follow-on is a 'design your own theme park' project. Near Barcelona there is a theme park which has a very 'Latin' theme with most of the park being based on Spanish or South American imagery and culture, a refreshing change to the near dominance of the American image in this kind of entertainment. Have students design a theme park which reflects their culture as well as their favourite rides or activities. In a mixed nationality class, each student can contribute a ride or show from their country.

2.45 Computer detectives

Aim:	To solve mysteries
Focus:	Predictions, reasoning, giving explanations
Level:	Upper-intermediate and above
Time:	75 minutes
Sites:	http://www.mysterynet.com

Procedure

Start off with a mystery of your own. My favourite is to describe the following scene: 'There is a man in the middle of a field; he is dead and has an unopened package next to him. What happened?'. Students are only allowed to ask questions which can be answered with 'yes' or 'no'. The answer is that he jumped from a plane, and the unopened package is his parachute. This is also a good opportunity to do some work on prediction, encouraging students to talk among themselves: 'he might have been…', 'perhaps he was…', etc.

Mystery Net has monthly and daily mysteries, so you'll have to look at the website just before you do the class. The See-N-Solve section (www.mysterynet.com/see/) has a crime story with a picture of the crime scene, so both textual and visual clues play a part. Choose a mystery and give students time to read it and discuss the clues before they take a look at the solution.

Examine how a typical mystery story is put together, trying to identify key parts: set the scene, introduce the characters, drop in a couple of clues to the identity of the criminal, the solution.

Use the picture from the Flash Mystery (http://www.mysterynet.com/flash/) to create group mystery stories, or supply pictures yourself from magazines or newspapers.

Variation

After telling your own mystery, encourage students to participate with any mysteries of their own which they may know. Alternatively, put them in pairs and invite them to make up their own mystery stories.

TIP ☑

Young learners can join in at http://kids.mysterynet.com or the Nancy Drew page http://nancy-drew.mysterynet.com. Extra ideas on working with mysteries at http://www.mysterynet.com/learn

---

2.46 Who said that … ?

Aim:	To learn some famous quotations
Focus:	Talking about famous people
Level:	Upper-intermediate and above
Time:	75 minutes
Sites:	http://www.famous-quotations.com/

Procedure

Start with the *Who said that … ?* activity. There's a good chance that your students will know some of them, but not all. Get feedback and see which ones they know, and what they know about the people who said them, and the circumstances in which they were said.

An alternative presentation might be to start by putting the names of the people from the *Who said that … ?* activity up on the board. Elicit any information about the people, and see if the students know what they are famous for. Then lead into the activity.

Give them time to finish the activity, finding the quotes they didn't know. Encourage quick finishers to look around, pointing out the different search options. Get feedback on the rest of the answers. Now tell them they are going to make an inspirational quotation wall, and that they have ten minutes to find two or three quotations each which they think are useful, funny, intelligent, etc.

Using large pieces of card or paper, have students make the quotations wall, discussing how quotations should be organised, and saying why they chose them and what meaning they have for them.

Who said that... ?

'We're more popular than Jesus Christ now.'
'Any colour, so long as it's black.'
'That's one small step for a man, one giant step for mankind.'
'I have a dream today.'
'All I need to make a comedy is a park, a policeman and a pretty girl.'
'It's often safer to be in chains than to be free.'
'Ask not what your country can do for you; ask what you can do for your country.'
'I never forget a face, but I'll make an exception in your case.'
'Hell is other people.'
'I cannot believe that God plays dice with the cosmos.'

Franz Kafka	Henry Ford	Groucho Marx
John Lennon	John F Kennedy	Martin Luther King
Neil Armstrong	Albert Einstein	Charles Chaplin
	Jean-Paul Sartre	

KEY (in order): John Lennon, Henry Ford, Neil Armstrong, Martin Luther King, Charles Chaplin, Franza Kafka, John F Kennedy, Groucho Marx, Jean-Paul Sartre, Albert Einstein

2.47 Waving the flag

Aim:	To learn about country names and flags
Focus:	Country names, colours, shapes
Level:	Elementary and above (young learners)
Time:	60 minutes
Sites:	http://www.photius.com/flags/flag_identifier.html

Procedure

Draw the flag of the country you teach in and get students to identify it. Then draw the flag of the country you come from (if different). Draw enough flags to illustrate the main designs used (vertical stripes, horizontal stripes, solid colours, etc.). You may need to do some work on the important vocabulary: colours, horizontal, vertical, slanting, narrow, broad, stripe, star, cross, crest, above, below, in the centre, in the corner, etc. Elicit all the country names your students know. Do they know what the flags look like? Encourage them to draw the flags on the board (with coloured chalks, perhaps) and describe them.

You'll need to guide students through a first use of the webpage. Choose Argentina, for example, and show them how to navigate through the interface: it's got horizontal stripes (they click on the link to the page with flags which have horizontal stripes) … three horizontal stripes … (they are blue and white, and there's a crest in the middle of the flag) and show them how to follow your description to get to the Argentinean flag. Now let them choose five flags they like and play the description game with a partner.

Lots of towns and cities have flags too. Print out the blank flag templates at the site and have students design a flag for the town or city you work in. What is the town famous for, and how could this be represented on a flag? This activity can also be applied to a flag for the school, the class, or even individuals. Have a competition to judge the best flag produced.

Follow-on

After going through the different designs flags can have, use the page which has small representations of all the flags (http://www.photius.com/flags/alphabetic_list.html) to play a game where someone describes a flag, and the rest of the class have to find it on the page. You could also prepare a 'Find a flag which …' game (e.g. 'Find a flag which has three horizontal stripes, red and yellow, with a crest.' [Spain]).

TIP ☑

The Flag Identifier uses a novel interface where you start with a basic idea, i.e. vertical or horizontal stripes, etc., and keep making choices until you get to the picture of the flag you are looking for. For more flags, see http://www.theodora.com/flags.html

---

2.48 Dream houses

Aim:	To design the perfect house
Focus:	Conditionals, housing vocabulary, descriptions
Level:	Advanced
Time:	90 minutes
Sites:	http://www.luxuryrealestate.com/
	http://www.eplans.com/article.hwx/Q/articleId.129106

Procedure

Start off the activity with the *Dream houses* discussion. Get some feedback on the discussion and try to establish common ground between all members of the class. You might like to do some preparatory revision work on language used for describing houses, prepositions, etc.

The Luxury Real Estate site has properties in varying price ranges. Divide students up into groups and give each group a different house. Give them time to tour their particular house, looking at all the photos and descriptions. Then put groups together and get them to give each other a guided tour of their houses using the photos and their own descriptions. Here they must imagine they are estate agents and are desperate to sell the house they are showing. Repeat this until everyone has seen all the houses. Get feedback and discuss the merits of each house.

Adapt the Eplans 'Questions to identify your needs in a plan' questionnaire and give students a little time to think about it and make notes. They then discuss it in pairs.

Variation

This activity could be adapted for lower levels by simply using the pictures from the different houses. These pictures feature all kinds of rooms and furniture which can easily be exploited at all levels.

Dream houses

If you had a lot of money and could design yourself a dream house, what would it be like? Think about the following factors, then compare in groups:

- house or apartment
- size, number and functions of rooms
- city centre, suburbs, countryside
- country or region
- exclusive area
- near to bus or train station
- space for entertaining
- space for working
- style of furniture and fittings
- extras: swimming pool, office, sauna, jacuzzi, air-conditioning, heating, etc.
- security
- privacy

© Cambridge University Press 2007

2.49 Net research

Aim:	To use the Internet for basic research
Focus:	Synonyms, rhymes, doing and reporting on research
Level:	Mid-intermediate and above
Time:	60 minutes
Sites:	http://www.itools.com

Procedure

Give out the *Net research* activity and give students time to look through it
and fill in any answers they can.

Take them to Research It! and show them the different sections, and how
to use them. This is an ideal opportunity to show students how to keep two
Internet browser windows open at the same time: one with the page they are
interested in, and another with a reference tool such as Research It! or the
translation page at AltaVista. This is easily achieved by opening Internet
Explorer or Firefox (in tabs) again and loading a different page. You can
then switch between them by clicking their respective buttons at the bottom
of your screen (or tabs, in Firefox). Show them how to switch between
windows, and also how to use the *Back* button on the browser to return to
the previous page.

Get feedback on the answers students have found and discuss their
experiences in using the Net this way. Is it useful? What are the advantages
and disadvantages of using the Net rather than traditional reference books?
How do they feel about reading from a computer screen?

Variation

You may need to vary this activity to suit your students. All the answers to
the activity below are easily available from the Research It! site.

If you teach students who speak one of the languages covered by the
AltaVista translation service, show students how to use it as a bilingual
dictionary whilst reading on the Net. Other translation options can be found
at http://www.logos.it

TIP ☑

See also the translation pages at AltaVista (http://babelfish.altavista.com).
For computing terminology see http://www.pcwebopaedia.com/

Net research

1 What is a scanner?
2 How many words do you know which rhyme with 'car'?
3 How many synonyms do you know for 'house'?
4 How do you say 'school' in Italian?
5 Can you think of an anagram for 'space'?
6 What does NATO stand for?
7 What is Volta famous for?
8 Who said 'All you need is love'?
9 What's the telephone code for Chicago in the USA?
10 How many Turkish lira can you get for US$25?

© Cambridge University Press 2007

2.50 Surveys 'R' us

Aim:	To get and give opinions
Focus:	Question forms, comparatives, superlatives
Level:	Elementary and above
Time:	60 minutes
Sites:	http://www.misterpoll.com/

Procedure

Start off with the *Surveys 'R' us* questionnaire. This one has been devised for upper-intermediate students, so you might need to make the level higher or lower depending on the group you are going to do this activity with. This simple survey will give students ideas on the kind of questionnaires they might want to put together later.

Make sure students see the difference between the types of question in the survey (multiple choice and 'either / or'). Put them into groups of three or four and give them time to think about the things they think are important. (This can be anything from politics to entertainment to what's happening or available in their home town.) Encourage them to design questionnaires with different types of questions.

Have them make their surveys on the website by filling in the forms and then get them to answer them themselves. Don't forget to make a note of the web addresses assigned to the finished surveys once you have created them online. Now get students from other groups to try each other's surveys.

The survey addresses can be advertised on the school or institution noticeboard and other classes invited to visit the computer facilities and vote. The surveys can also be printed and used offline in a speaking activity.

Follow-on

Write to EFL listservs (see *Section 4*) and advertise your new surveys, inviting teachers and students to visit them and vote. Post results to the list at a later date. The surveys prepared online can (if printed) be the basis of a lively debate in class.

TIP ☑

This activity is easily adapted to very low levels where the subject can be food, drink, colours, animals, etc. You may also need to update the survey by changing celebrities' names.

Surveys 'R' us

1 Who's the best actor?
   a) Brad Pitt b) Pierce Brosnan c) Keanu Reeves d) Sean Connery

2 Who's the best singer?
   a) Bono b) Paul McCartney c) Mick Jagger d) Damon Albarn

3 What would you do with $1 million?
   a) Spend it b) Save it c) Give it to charity

4 What's the most expensive restaurant in town?
   a) .... b) .... c) .... d) ....

5 How old are you?
   a) under 20 b) under 30 c) under 40 d) under 50 e) under 60

6 What sex are you?
   a) male b) female

7 Do you like learning English?
   a) Yes b) No

2.51 Survival

Aim: To learn about survival techniques and advice
Focus: Advice, instructions, imperatives
Level: Upper-intermediate and above
Time: 60 minutes
Sites: http://www.safetycentral.com/disprep.html

Procedure

The Disaster Preparedness Guides have lots of useful advice on how to survive diverse disasters such as earthquakes, flooding, hurricanes, landslides, fire, thunderstorms, tornadoes, volcanoes, etc. Choose the ones you feel are most appropriate and divide the class into groups, allocating a disaster to each group. Have them brainstorm what to do in the event of the disaster, dividing the activity into before, during and after. Get feedback as a class.

Give students time to look through their section, check what they thought of, and add to the advice from the information they find there.

As a class, go through the advice found on the different pages. Design a general disaster preparedness list with this information.

Survival

Your ship is sinking next to a desert island. It is very hot and there is no shade or fresh water. You have time to grab ten things from the boat. Decide which things you would take, and why:

A big sheet of plastic	10 boxes of matches
2 bottles of whisky	An overcoat
A torch	A gun with 20 bullets
A mirror	Sunglasses
A map	8 litres of water
A radio with batteries	A compass
A first-aid kit	A knife
A portable computer	2 chickens
A magnifying glass	An empty bottle
A ball of string	A spade

© Cambridge University Press 2007

Follow-on

The information gathered could be turned into a colourful 'Warning!' poster, illustrated with pictures and practising some of the more usual structures found in this context: direct imperatives (dos and don'ts), advice and suggestions (try to…, make sure you…, etc.).

Alternatively, try the *Survival* activity. This can be done as a simple discussion about priorities and uses. Are any of the items potentially more dangerous than helpful? Which items could be put to more than one use? A good example is the ball of string which could be used for making a raft (if wood was found) or for tying the overcoat up as a makeshift shelter.

2.52 Teen spirit

Aim:	To talk about teenage life and issues
Focus:	Teenage problems
Level:	Mid-intermediate and above
Time:	60 minutes
Sites:	http://www.teenmag.com/ http://www.theinsite.org / http://www.teenpeople.com

Procedure
Start with a general brainstorm of teenage issues – what are the most important issues and themes of teenage life? Some of the issues raised could include: music, parents, liberty, education, career, sexuality, going out, shopping, friends, etc. What are the main problems teenagers have?

The websites in the notes to this activity are all produced by teenagers for teenagers. They are large, diverse sites, and as such are not ideally suited to planning an exact class. I have used them with the website review form (see *Activity 2.55 Reviewing a website*) to engage students in a discussion of which sites might be useful for finding like-minded people. Alternatively, give students time to look through them and then have a class discussion about the interesting things they found whilst browsing.

If your students don't find anything useful in these sites, have them visit the teenage section of Yahoo! http://dir.yahoo.com/Society_and_Culture/ Cultures_and_Groups/Teenagers/

Discuss the sites found – which ones were interesting, which ones boring, etc. Have students write up a clean copy of the website review form (see *Appendix A*) for later reference. This is an ideal opportunity to start a class website review file if you do not already keep one.

Follow-on
There is plenty of opportunity here for a more wide-ranging discussion on the position of teenagers and adolescents in society. You might like to touch

upon the subject of the clash between teenagers and adults, the different attitudes to teenage boys and girls in some societies, etc.

2.53 What's in a name?

Aim:	To find out about people's names
Focus:	Names and their meanings
Level:	Lower-intermediate and above
Time:	75 minutes
Sites:	http://www.behindthename.com

Procedure

Start with the *Famous names* activity. Get feedback and discuss why people change their names. Are students happy with theirs?

Give out a list of all the names of people in the class. Give everyone a chance to find their name on the Behind The Name site. Then do a walkround activity with everyone asking *What's your name?* and *What does it mean?*. If some students don't find their name, encourage them to use Yahoo! or Google for further searching.

Now ask students to think about what they would like their name to be if they were famous. They can used the Random Name Generator on the site to invent new names. Encourage students to be adventurous and find themselves a new identity. Make sure they find out the significance of their new name too.

Now do a further walkround activity with students using their new identities, asking and answering the same questions as before (i.e . *What's your name?* and *What does it mean?*).

Follow-on

A good written follow-on would be for students to interview one of the new famous people and write up the interview.

KEY: Bernard Schwartz – Tony Curtis; Rogers Nelson – Prince; Dino Paul Crocetti – Dean Martin; Frances Gumm – Judy Garland; Marion Michael Morrison – John Wayne; George O'Dowd – Boy George; Eric Arthur Blair – George Orwell; Georgios Panayiotou – George Michael; Thomas Conner – Sean Connery; David Jones – David Bowie; Norma Jean Baker – Marilyn Monroe; Paul Hewson – Bono; Reginald Dwight – Elton John; Gordon Sumner – Sting

---

Famous names

Can you match the original name of these famous people on the left with their stage names on the right?

Bernard Schwartz	Sting
Rogers Nelson	Bono
Dino Paul Crocetti	Elton John
Frances Gumm	Marilyn Monroe
Marion Michael Morrison	John Wayne
George O'Dowd	George Michael
Eric Arthur Blair	Tony Curtis
Georgios Panayiotou	Dean Martin
Thomas Conner	Sean Connery
David Jones	David Bowie
Norma Jean Baker	Boy George
Paul Hewson	George Orwell
Reginald Dwight	Prince
Gordon Sumner	Judy Garland

© Cambridge University Press 2007

2.54 Inventions and discoveries

Aim: To talk about inventions which have changed our lives
Focus: Passives, past tenses
Level: Upper-intermediate and above
Time: 60 minutes
Sites: http://www.indianchild.com/inventions.htm

Procedure

Brainstorm a list of inventions and discoveries which students think have changed people's lives. Try to get ten up on the board, then get students to put them in order of importance. Which ones could they live without, and which not? Now do the *Inventions and discoveries* activity.

Students can check their answers on the Famous Inventions site. Take the inventions and discoveries the students thought were important and distribute them round groups. Have students find out something more about the person who invented or discovered it – biographical details, other inventions, etc. (see the Biographical Dictionary at http://www.s9.com for resources). Early finishers should be encouraged to wander round the website looking at anyone else who interests them.

Students share what they have found out about the inventors and discoverers. Which one was the most prolific? Which was the most important?

Variation

For work on the passive, consider broadening the categories to take in paintings, buildings, discoveries, inventions, records, films, etc., thus allowing for a wider range of verbs (discover, invent, paint, direct, build, design, etc.).

Follow-on

A good follow-on activity is to talk about things which haven't been invented yet. Have students make a list of things which have been talked about, but not yet built, e.g. flying cars, teleportation, space colonies, etc. What would they like to live to see? What do they think are going to be the most important advances over the coming years?

Work on writing biographies of famous inventors and discoverers can also make a good follow-on activity.

Inventions and discoveries

Can you match the invention/discovery with the person?

Kodak camera	Alfred Nobel
Light bulb	Josephine Cochrane
Dynamite	Alexander Fleming
Windscreen wiper	George Eastman
Frozen food	John Logie Baird
Dishwasher	Thomas Edison
Television	Clarence Birdseye
Penicillin	Chester Carlson
World Wide Web	Mary Anderson

Do you know when these things were invented/discovered?
Which of these do you think are important?
Which of them could you do without?

© Cambridge University Press 2007

KEY: Alfred Nobel – Dynamite, 1867; Josephine Cochrane – Dishwasher, 1886; Alexander Fleming – Penicillin, 1928; George Eastman – Kodak camera, 1888; John Logie Baird – Television, 1926; Thomas Edison – Light bulb, 1879; Clarence Birdseye – Frozen food, 1924; Tim Berners Lee – World Wide Web, 1989; Mary Anderson – Windscreen wiper, 1903

2.55 Reviewing a website

Aim:	To learn how to review and classify websites
Focus:	Adjectives, language used for reviewing
Level:	Elementary and above
Time:	60 minutes
Sites:	No specific sites

Procedure

Have a group discussion about good websites students have visited. Get some addresses and talk about what made them good: was it the content, the presentation, or something else? Build up a set of criteria for reviewing websites. This can be done by simply taking students' ideas or by using the website review form (see *Appendix A*). Note that the website review form is designed for teacher use, so it will need some adaptation. You will also need to find examples of websites for later review – use ones from your own surfing.

Put students in small groups and get each member in turn to give the other members of the group a quick tour of a website they like, pointing out the best features and explaining why it is good. Remind students at this point how to *Bookmark* or add a site to the *Favorites*. Now give out blank review forms and ask students to visit one or two sites and review them. Make sure they know that the forms they fill in must make sense to other people reading them later.

Share the newly-created reviews around the class, discussing the websites visited. Establish a class folder for website information and decide together how to classify the website review forms. It's a good idea to appoint someone to look after the folder and make sure it is up-to-date. This will, over time, become an invaluable resource for the whole class.

3   Tools for Online Work

In this section we'll be taking a look at how you and your students can use various Internet tools and how they can publish their own work on the Web. The first couple of projects revolve around email exchanges. Later projects are based on webpages and the section looks briefly at other common Internet collaboration tools.

3.1 Email projects and discussion lists

With most teachers and students being familiar with email these days, this is an ideal medium for getting your classes interacting with other students around the world. One of the best ways of doing this is by organising an email penpal exchange with other students in another country. This is immensely motivating for students, as the combination of technology, speed of communication and writing for a 'real' audience combine to provide the sort of experience which is difficult to create in the classroom alone.

Starting off
Before entering into any commitment to do a penpal exchange, you may find it necessary to spend some time teaching your students how to write, send and receive email, etc. It is not advisable to try to teach these basic skills at the same time as you ask them to write to their partners. Spending some time on email skills before starting the exchange will help you to avoid problems once it is under way. When you have done the groundwork, it's time to think about how to get an exchange going.

There are plenty of EFL sites on the Net which have penpal pages, and it's a good idea to have a look at these sites first, just to get some idea of what people are doing. One nice penpal site is at http://its-myworld.com where students can leave messages and answer messages left by other would-be writers. Here's how to introduce the activity:

a Give students a chance to browse the penpals.
b Give them the *Electronic penpals* activity and let them find the answers.
c Get feedback and ask students which two people they've decided to write to.

d   Spend some time working on a good introductory message. This should include information about themselves, where they live and what they do, their interests, likes and dislikes, etc.

e   Send the messages.

Electronic penpals

Find someone ...

- from the same country as you ....
- from a country you'd like to visit ....
- the same age and sex as you ....
- with similar interests to you ....

Find someone who ...

- wouldn't like to hear from you! ....
- likes something you've never heard of ....
- does something you'd like to do ....
- likes a band you like ....

Find ...

- an Internet word for 'email penpal' ....
- a spelling mistake you can correct ....
- someone you definitely wouldn't write to ....
- two people you'd love to write to ....

© Cambridge University Press 2007

This can be a very stimulating exercise and excellent practice for most students. There is, however, a down side. Many individuals put penpal messages on more than one site. Often they get too many messages and decide not to bother replying, or they decide on one person who really interests them and ignore the rest. It can be a very disheartening experience to excitedly check your mail every day, waiting for a response and never getting one, so it is best to warn students in advance that there are no guarantees.

TIP ☑

You can get more advice on how to find penpals and how to set up an email exchange at the website which accompanies this book. Visit the website at http://www.cambridge.org/elt/chlt/internet and look for the email section.

Finding partners

If its-myworld doesn't have the sort of people you are looking for, there are
plenty of other penpal sites – for more addresses, see *Section 5* at the end of
the book.

The best penpal exchanges work class to class. And the best way to find a
class with which to exchange is to advertise on one of the email mailing lists
(listservs) such as TESL-L or NETEACH-L. (See *Section 4*.)

Guidelines

Where I used to work in Barcelona, Spain, we had a very successful exchange
for two years with a school in the US. Their students were studying Spanish,
so we ran a bilingual exchange: our students wrote 70% English and 30%
Spanish, their US counterparts did the opposite. This helped both groups
immensely, as it gave them a chance really to express themselves – at least for
part of each letter – and often to include the type of language we as teachers
tend not to cover in the classroom.

A good exchange will depend on many factors. Here are some
considerations:

1   Find a teacher in your partner school who understands the technology
    and is committed to the exchange.
2   Match each student up with two or more in the partner school. This
    means that if people leave, or are absent for a while, each student will at
    least have one person to write to.
3   If they do not already have one, give students access to individual email
    accounts. If the place where you teach does not have the resources for
    this, try using one of the free web-based email services such as Hotmail
    http://www.hotmail.com. For more information, see the website list in
    Section 5 of this book. Bear in mind, however, that free web-based email
    services are often quite slow.
4   Prepare your students carefully: point out that email still takes time to
    arrive, that some people write more quickly and reply sooner than others.
    Be prepared for the occasions when some students don't have a letter to
    reply to.
5   Point out that cultural differences are important, and that allowances
    must be made when writing to people abroad. We once had an
    unfortunate incident with the translation of a Spanish swear word which
    is inoffensive in Spanish, yet rather stronger in English. These matters can
    be dealt with as they arise.

6 Try to establish a program of message content, whilst not disturbing your students' natural desire to communicate. I have found that a simple task for each letter (e.g. describe a typical school day in your country, a typical day at work, etc.) helps to give focus to the writing. Each message can be divided into carrying out the task, and a section for whatever the student wants to write about.

With some careful planning, and a good partner school, you can easily set up and run a very successful exchange. Here are notes on two example exchanges (between two countries) with which I have been involved in the last couple of years:

Sample exchange 1

This exchange was between a school of English in Spain and a secondary school in Milton Keynes, UK where the students study Spanish. Initially, two classes of twelve students between 13 and 15 years old were paired up and the exchange, which started in October, had the following program:

- Students in both countries sent off a brief description of themselves in both languages (Spanish and English). The messages were designed to look more or less like a typical penfriend advert in a magazine.
- Students were then allocated two partners in the other country, bearing in mind any preferences wherever possible.
- One set of students made the first contact with a letter of introduction and details of Christmas in their country. The other students replied before the Christmas holidays with a similar message.
- From January onwards, students were encouraged to make contact at least once a month, with the teachers suggesting possible topics for inclusion in their messages. They were encouraged to write about the topic and then move on to whatever personal content they wanted to include.

Sample exchange 2

This exchange was with the same school as exchange 1, but for higher level students in both schools. The project concentrated on items of news and social topics with the following program:

- On the first of every month, the teachers decided together on a topic of world interest, and separately on a topic of national interest.
- By the 10th of each month, the students sent off any information they had gathered (usually from the Internet and local sources of news) related to these two topics. This information was sent in the students' own

language, and they undertook to provide vocabulary glossaries and explanations where necessary.

- During the following ten days the material received was used in class by the teachers, and students compared reactions in both countries to the item of world news, as well as learning what was important to their partners on a national scale.
- In the final third of the month, students sent and received messages in which they talked about their reactions to the news items and had the opportunity to ask follow-up questions, as well as 'socialise'.

Note: At the end of each month the students got together on a text chat system to 'talk' to each other in a group debate. These sessions were saved to disk and used as follow-on material later.

Variations

COMMUNITY BOX

An interesting add-on to a penpal exchange is to arrange for you and your partner school to exchange 'Community boxes' – boxes (either real and full of real objects, or 'virtual', with scanned images, brochures, etc.) of information and realia from your country or area. This can become quite a large project, with groups of students working on different aspects of life in the area, and is a great way to stimulate interest from both groups.

EMAIL EXCHANGE TIPS

1 Don't underestimate the time students will want to spend on writing their messages. You might be surprised at how much more effort they put into writing to their partners than they usually do when writing for you. Don't take it to heart – it is usually much more exciting for them than a more traditional writing exercise!
2 If you are short of time in the classroom and don't want to (or can't) spend a whole lesson writing messages, have students write them at home and look over them at the beginning of the next class. Students with computers at home can even type the messages and bring them in on disk, thus saving even more time. Alternatively, have them send you their messages by email for you to comment on and return.
3 Remember, this is not an exam composition, so there is probably no need to insist on total accuracy. Besides anything else, too much correction

may inhibit students' desire to communicate and will take the fun out of the project.

4 As with accuracy, insisting on the content of messages will not allow your students to establish a real relationship with the people they are writing to. I've found that breaking the message exchange down into two components – task (a set topic students have to write about first) and free writing – gives some focus to each assignment whilst allowing everyone time and space to express themselves.

5 As you saw in *Section 1*, email messages are usually written in a very informal way – don't insist on your students writing 'model compositions' during an email exchange. This is an area worth exploring with your students, and you may need to work on raising their awareness of the differences between acceptable writing in email format as opposed to that which is more appropriate for formal written communications. It may even be worth spending a class on identifying what is normal in email communications, but not acceptable in formal writing: abbreviations, phrases rather than sentences, missing punctuation, emoticons, etc.

Student discussion lists and forums

Another excellent way to get learners involved in writing is to have them subscribe to a discussion list or partake in a forum. Both of these resources involve real, meaningful communication – sometimes with other learners, sometimes with native speakers.

The SL-Lists are a good place to start. Set up in 1994, they are co-hosted by La Trobe University in Australia and Kyoto Sangyo University in Japan. There are several different lists for your learners to choose from:

INTRO-SL	Discussion List for New Members
CHAT-SL	General Discussion List (Low level)
DISCUSS-SL	General Discussion List (High level)
BUSINESS-SL	Discussion List on Business and Economics
ENGL-SL	Discussion List on Learning English
EVENT-SL	Discussion List on Current Events
MOVIE-SL	Discussion List on the Cinema
MUSIC-SL	Discussion List on Music
SCITECH-SL	Discussion List on Science, Technology & Computers
SPORT-SL	Discussion List on Sports

More information can be found at http://www.kyoto-su.ac.jp/~trobb/slinfo.html

These lists can be used as extra-curricular resources for more autonomous learners, but you might like to dedicate a couple of sessions to getting your classes signed up, showing them how they work, and encouraging the first couple of posts. Once you've been through the basics with them, the interested students should find plenty of opportunities for interaction. More list resources (both for teachers and learners) can be found on this page at the University of Oregon http://babel.uoregon.edu/yamada/lists/english.html

Learner forums function similarly, although it is more usual to visit the forum webpage than to interact purely by email. The English Forums site (http://www.englishforums.com/) is a vibrant example of such a community, with over 30,000 visits per day at the time of writing. The English Club site (http://www.englishclub.com/esl-forums/index.php) has a collection divided into learning resources and general interest forums, and you can find plenty of forum activity at Dave Sperling's ESL Café (http://www.eslcafe.com/forums/student/index.php).

Again, you might like to spend some time with your learners, perhaps organising an introductory activity based around their interests, so that they get comfortable with the forums, how they work, and the types of postings that are acceptable.

Dave Sperling's ESL Café forums

1 Look at these topics: *computers   current news   culture   family   film & cinema   health & fitness   hobbies   holidays   literature   music   pets   science   sport   travel*

2 Choose two you are interested in and write them on a piece of paper.

3 Exchange your paper with a partner. Visit the forums related to your partner's interests and read some of the recent postings. Prepare a quiz for your partner to do.

4 Do the quiz your partner prepares for you. If you don't know the right answers, post messages to your two forums to find out more.

© Cambridge University Press 2007

This simple activity will get them in to the forums, and – hopefully – posting a couple of messages and getting replies to them. Again, you may not want to spend too much class time on this kind of activity, but if you can get your learners into forums such as the Dave's ESL Café ones, they may return in their own time to interact with other learners and teachers around the world.

3.2 Webquests

An introduction

Bernie Dodge of San Diego State University was one of the first people to attempt to define and structure this kind of learning activity. According to him, a webquest is 'an inquiry-oriented activity in which some or all of the information that learners interact with comes from resources on the Internet …'. He identifies two types of webquests:

Short-term webquests The instructional goal of a short-term webquest is knowledge acquisition and integration. At the end of a short-term webquest, a learner will have grappled with a significant amount of new information and made sense of it.

Longer-term webquests The instructional goal of a longer-term webquest is extending and refining knowledge. After completing a longer-term webquest, a learner will have analysed a body of knowledge deeply, transformed it in some way, and demonstrated an understanding of the material by creating something that others can respond to, online or offline.

This definition has been refined over the years, and adapted for various different disciplines. Philip Benz (owner of the English Multiverse) describes a webquest as follows: 'A webquest is a constructivist approach to learning (…). Students not only collate and organize information they've found on the Web, they orient their activities towards a specific goal they've been given, often associated with one or more roles modeled on adult professions. Since students have to participate in the elaboration of their learning strategies, the level of autonomy and creative production they attain is increased. With the proper guidance and "scaffolding" students can accomplish far more actual learning than in traditional transmission-of-knowledge situations that so often leave them wishing they were anywhere but in the classroom.'

Essentially, then, we might consider webquests to be mini-projects in which a large percentage of the input and material is supplied by the Internet. Webquests can be teacher-made or learner-made, depending on the learning activity the teacher decides on.

There are many compelling reasons for using webquests in the classroom, including:

* They are an easy way for teachers to begin to incorporate the Internet into the language classroom, on both a short-term and long-term basis – no specialist technical knowledge is needed either to produce or use them.

- More often than not, they are group activities and as a result they lend themselves to communication and the sharing of knowledge – two principal goals of language teaching itself. The use of webquests encourages cooperative learning, and therefore stimulates conversation.
- They can be used simply as a linguistic tool, but can also be interdisciplinary, allowing for cross-over into other departments and subject areas (where applicable). This can often give them a more 'real-world' look and feel and provide greater motivation for the learner.
- They encourage critical (or higher level) thinking skills, including: comparing, classifying, inducing, deducing, analysing errors, constructing support, abstraction, analysing perspectives, etc. Learners are not able simply to regurgitate information they find, but are guided towards a transformation of that information in order to achieve a given task.
- They are both motivating and authentic tasks (if well-designed) and encourage learners to view the activities they are doing as something 'real' or 'useful'. This inevitably leads to more effort, greater concentration and a real interest in task achievement. This, coupled with real-life material and input, can be a greater motivator than routine teaching materials.

Webquests have now been around long enough for them to have a clearly-defined structure. However, this structure – whilst being unofficially recognised as the definitive schema for these activities – should only really be taken as a basic guideline and you should design your webquests to suit the needs and learning styles of your group.

There are usually four main sections to a webquest and you will see how these work together in the samples suggested below:

1 **Introduction**
   This stage is normally used to introduce the overall theme of the webquest. It involves giving background information on the topic and, in the language learning context, often introduces key vocabulary and concepts which learners will need to understand in order to complete the tasks involved.
2 **Task**
   This section of the webquest explains clearly and precisely what the learners will have to do as they work their way through the webquest. The task should obviously be highly motivating and intrinsically interesting for the learners, and should be firmly anchored in a real-life

situation. This often involves the learners in a certain amount of role-play within a given scenario (e.g. you are the school social organiser and have to organise a trip for your class to an English-speaking country ...).

3 **Process**

The third stage of a webquest guides the learners through certain activities and research tasks, using a set of pre-defined resources. These resources are predominantely web-based, and are usually presented in clickable form within the task document (it's important to bear in mind that it's much easier to click on a link than to type it in with any degree of accuracy). In the case of a language-based webquest, this stage of the webquest may introduce (or recycle) lexical areas or grammatical points which are essential to the task. The process stage of the webquest will usually have one (or sometimes several) 'products' which the learners are expected to present at the end and which will often form the basis of the final, evaluation stage.

4 **Evaluation**

This stage can involve learners in self-evaluation, comparing and contrasting what they have produced with other learners and giving feedback on what they feel they have learnt, achieved, etc. It will also involve teacher-evaluation of the same, and good webquests will give guidance to the teacher for this particular part of the process. For a good example of this, see the 'Who Made My Trainers?' webquest below.

Since Bernie Dodge developed his model in 1995, many educators have added both to the theory and the practice of webquests, and it is now possible to find several good examples of them in many different subject areas. Take a look at two examples:

Who Made My Trainers? How to be a Responsible Consumer
http://www.xtec.es/crle/02/webquests/english/2index2.html
New York! New York!
http://www.onestopenglish.com/section.asp?theme=mag&catid=58218&docid=145587

Note that both these webquests are teacher-designed, and only one of them adheres strictly to the structure set out above. However, both models engage the learners in collaborative tasks, thus promoting communication.

Before sitting down to plan a webquest, it is always worth searching around on the Net to see if someone has produced something which might fit your needs. There are plenty of webquest 'repositories' out on the Net (see http://www.theconsultants-e.com/webquests/ for one example), so there is little point in re-inventing the wheel. Use Google to have a good look around before you do the hard work yourself.

In the event that you do have to design and produce your own webquest, these guidelines will get you started:

1 Define the topic area and the end product (introduction and task stages).
2 Find web resources which are suitable content-wise and linguistically.
3 Group the resources according to stages of the task.
4 Structure the process – tasks, resources, lexical areas, grammatical areas.
5 Design the evaluation stages and concepts.

Once these guidelines have been followed, the webquest can be put together as a simple word processed document (add images and links to all the resources learners will need) or as a webpage – this can be hosted on a school server or one of the free services such as Geocities, Tripod, etc. (See *Section 5* for more details.)

> Further information on webquests can be found here:
> http://webquest.sdsu.edu/about_webquests.html
> http://www.ardecol.ac-grenoble.fr/english/tice/enwebquests.htm
> http://tommarch.com/learning/index.php
> http://www.webquest.org/
> http://www.feo.hvu.nl/koen2/Talenquest/index-l.htm
> http://members.aol.com/adrmoser/tips/mwq.html

3.3 Blogs and wikis

Blogs

Blogs (an abbreviation for 'web-logs') originally served the function of online diaries kept by individual Internet users. Early blogs were simply text reflections shared by their writers, often with links to other sites the author found useful. A typical blog would appear as a simple webpage composed of a collection of small articles, with additional links. Older messages would be archived at the end of each two-week or monthly period.

Over time – and particularly in educational contexts, where research is just beginning to take off – they have become tools for collaboration, information exchange and reflection, to the extent that there are now various models of blogging.

The Internet and the Language Classroom

Graham Stanley (http://www.teachingenglish.org.uk/think/resources/blogging.shtml) describes three types of blog in educational contexts, from the tutor blog (run by a teacher, usually for informational purposes), through the class blog (a space where teachers and learners can collaborate) to the learner blog (an individual blog for each learner).

In my current professional context (online teacher training and development), I use blogs with my course participants as reflective journals, giving them the time and space to consider the work they are doing online, to reflect on the process and the product, and to provide a one-to-one space for problem solving and consultation.

There are plenty of places which allow you to set up free blogs, but perhaps the best known, and easiest to use, is Blogger (http://www.blogger.com) where you can host any number of blogs, as long as you don't mind the advertising which comes with the free service.

Further information on blogs and blogging for EFL can be found here:

http://blog-efl.blogspot.com/
http://webpages.csus.edu/~hansonsm/Blogging.html

http://dekita.org/articles/classroom-blogging-two-fundamental-approaches
http://writing.berkeley.edu/tesl-ej/ej35/m1.html
http://www.grahamstanley.com/weblogs/

Wikis

By contrast, a wiki is more akin to a collaborative website tool, allowing multiple users to add pages to a website without any specialist knowledge. The most famous wiki ('wiki' is Hawaiian for 'fast', or an acronym for 'what I know is …' depending on which sources you consult) is Wikipedia (http://www.wikipedia.org), an online encyclopaedia which has been developed over recent years, and is now said to rival its more august print competitors such as the Encyclopaedia Britannica. The entries, though they may be inserted by anyone, are vetted by readers, so you can't insert unreliable information and get away with it, with unreliable entries often being corrected in as little as five minutes of being posted.

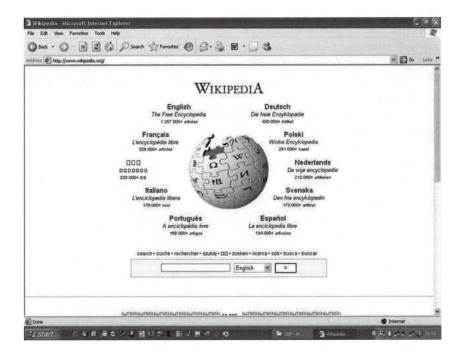

A wiki will allow any number of users to add any number of pages to it, and these pages can be interlinked. Additionally, pages can be edited by all users, and at any time.

A wiki is an ideal place for collaborative writing projects involving classes, or multinational student groups and worth considering as an alternative to the class or learner blog solutions mentioned above. It is also an excellent space in which to work through writing projects as a series of writing, editing, revision, etc., stages and this lends itself perfectly to the process writing approach.

To get started with a free wiki, try Wikispaces at http://www.wikispaces.com/
Further information on wikis and EFL can be found here:

http://www.irrodl.org/index.php/irrodl
http://careo.elearning.ubc.ca/wiki?WikiLand
http://edweb.sdsu.edu/courses/edtec700/wiki/

3.4 Online groups

An introduction

Online groups are a natural extension to some of the other tools already mentioned in this section. Forming groups will allow not only the sharing of thoughts in simple text format, but also uploading of files and photos, chatrooms and polls, calendars of events and other elements designed to turn a collection of individuals with a shared interest into a functioning online community.

Perhaps the best known online groups are Yahoo! Groups
http://groups.yahoo.com

There are online groups for learners and for teachers, as well as groups covering every other subject you can imagine. Groups such as these can provide a real alternative to the student lists mentioned above, but be aware that most groups are for native speakers, and so may prove difficult for your learners. Having said this, Yahoo! enforces a strict classification for the groups, separating the 'adult' groups from the others, and this can prove beneficial in the teaching context.

Here is what a typical group front page looks like – notice the group elements in the left-hand menu:

Below you'll find a simple task file to get your learners started exploring Yahoo! Groups.

Yahoo! Groups

1 Find a Yahoo! Group …
- about a subject you're interested in. Make sure it's possible to join without a moderator having to accept you.
- where the messages are either publicly available or available to members (not hidden completely).
- which has been active in the last two weeks (at least two or three messages per week).

2 Now subscribe to the group. Read through some of the messages, then try to answer the following questions about the group:
- What is the title of the group?
- What is its aim, and who are the intended members?
- How many members does it have?
- Is it a permanent group or does it have a specified beginning and end?
- Is there a leader of any kind – or is it a completely open group of equals?

© Cambridge University Press 2007

Apart from joining existing groups, you can, of course, set up your own groups with Yahoo! Groups. You could investigate this possibility if you want a private group for a particular class or project, or to build a community with your students outside their normal class time. To get started, go to http://groups.yahoo.com/start

3.5 Chat

The term *chat* – when it is used in the field of the Internet – refers to synchronous (i.e. real time) communication between two or more people, using the keyboard as the means of communication. This can be contrasted with voice chat, which allows two people to *speak* to each other using the Internet, as with a normal telephone call.

In this section we will be briefly considering these two ways of communicating in real time and looking at some of the available tools.

In terms of text chat, one can either use a specially designed program, such as Microsoft Messenger to interact with a person or a group of people in other locations, or one can join a web-based chat room dedicated to the EFL community.

Dave's ESL Café hosts a relatively good chat service, which you can find here: http://www.eslcafe.com/chat/chatpro.cgi Your learners will need to register, but this does tend to ensure that the users are genuinely interested in chatting in English and will allow your group to interact with other learners. However, it will mean that they are in a public room, which is not controlled by a teacher. Despite this, they will find plenty of opportunities to talk with other learners around the world, discuss current affairs or any other topic they decide to initiate. As the teacher, you can make good use of the transcripts afterwards to do some language work, should you choose.

Outside of the world of ELT they will often find more vibrant chat communities, but there is more potential for chaos and offence. If you decide to take your learners to such spaces, please make sure that they are aware of the basic safety tips:

- people on the Internet may not be who they say they are;
- never give out personal details (location, email address, etc.);
- don't share personal information about friends and family;
- never meet anyone you have met in an online chat, unless you are sure of who they are.

The initial experience for most learners will be one of bewilderment, and their ability to interact on any meaningful level will be determined by various factors. They will have to be able to think fast and type quickly and accurately, and also to pick apart multiple topic threads and distinguish between different ongoing 'conversations'. Public chat rooms can be found at http://chat.yahoo.com. At the time of writing, the ability to create your own rooms is disabled, but they are said to be re-establishing it soon.

For more work-based chat opportunities (such as an extra communication channel for an email exchange, for example) this ability to have your own private room will be vital. Private chats between two groups of learners can be a much more effective way of using the chat medium, and I have had some very successful chats over the years. I particularly enjoyed an ongoing project between my centre in Barcelona and a centre in Poland where we met once a week (one class in each country) to talk about issues of relevance to both groups. Each chat was structured so that the first half had a purpose and a focus – making it easier for the learners to get to grips with the medium and the language – and the second was free time, allowing them to get to know each other better. For this we used Microsoft Comic Chat, and whilst it is no longer officially supported, you can download it and get connected using the information found here http://www.mermeliz.com/cchat.htm

For more information on web-based chat in ELT, take a look at this article by Teresa Almeida d'Eça http://www-writing.berkeley.edu/TESL-EJ/ej25/int.html

Getting away from web-based chat and into a more controlled environment, you might like to consider Microsoft Messenger (http://messenger.msn.com). Each of your learners will need a Microsoft Passport ID to register and use the software, but you will then be able to set up private chat rooms between a number of learners, and – given fast enough connections – take advantage of the voice chat facility, with (optionally) webcam which enables participants to see each other. Messenger also allows for file sharing. Recent versions of Messenger can be set up to log chat sessions – again allowing for later language work.

In the same vein, Skype (http://www.skype.com) also does both text and voice chat and, like Messenger, is free to download and use.

Web-based chats and programs such as those mentioned above can, of course, be used in place of the more traditional email approach in a student penpal exchange. Live chat is in many ways more satisfying than sending and waiting for messages by email. However, if you choose this option, you should be aware that there are far more things that can go wrong, from not being able to get a connection to the Internet (and that could happen at either end of the operation) to not being able to control the language produced on all the computers.

3.6 Writing projects

Getting students published

There are plenty of opportunities for your students to publish their writing on the Net. Not only does this give them an immense feeling of satisfaction and pride in their work, but it also encourages them to take more time over presentation, accuracy, etc. One such place is the student magazine called TOPICS (http://www.topics-mag.com/index.html). Published four times a year, this magazine has features, articles and stories from learners worldwide.

All this can be done by having students prepare and type up their articles, then mailing them to the submission address found at the website. There's no limit to what you can send, so it's another ideal opportunity for doing an extended project. The great difference here is that the final audience for the project work is enormous.

More information on student writing can be found here http://www.topics-mag.com/onlinemag/welcome.htm

---

TIP ☑

There is often a lot of discussion and disagreement about the 'ethical' aspects of putting student work on the Net, with regard to copyright and the publication of information about students.

Most people agree that it is sensible to have students (or their parents or legal guardians) sign a release form – giving the school or institution permission to publish student writing – before publishing their work. A sample release form is provided as a guideline in *Appendix B*. It will probably need adapting for your purposes and place of work.

A step further in this process is to help your learners write and prepare their work in the form of webpages or mini-websites. This can be particularly useful when none of the existing sites suits the type of writing project you're running, or simply for publishing on a school web server.

It is beyond the scope of this book to teach teachers how to make complicated webpages, but the examples in this section are all very easy and straightforward. You will find these sample projects and advice on how to

write webpages at the website which accompanies the book, at
http://www.cambridge.org/elt/chlt/internet

Whilst you can immediately make use of the email based projects above, it would be advisable to visit the website and have a good look at the examples before attempting to put together a webpage with your students. You can find more information about websites which help with making webpages in *Section 5* of this book.

Getting students involved in actually producing webpages and putting them up on the Net is a wonderful way of letting them share their thoughts, culture and customs with other people around the world. Obviously, projects such as these work best if there is some kind of collaboration between countries, but simple pages which allow for feedback from the person visiting them will work well too.

The activities in this section vary in length from a simple class activity to an extended project over a considerable amount of time. Most of them can be made very easily using the HTML possibilities of any modern word processor or text editor. Where extra software or skills are necessary, you will find pointers to relevant resources.

TIP ☑

It is potentially dangerous to publish personal information about people on the Internet. This is particularly true when working with children and young learners. Publishing names, addresses, contact information and photographs of such groups of people should be done with great care (if at all) and with permission of a parent or legal guardian. When in doubt, it is better to err on the side of caution.

There are templates (a template is a rough model for a webpage, and contains common elements, titles and pictures, etc. which can be used as starting points for making websites) and example files for most of these projects on the book website at http://www.cambridge.org/elt/chlt/internet

It would be a good idea to start with the templates and work with them for a while. They have been kept deliberately simple to understand and adapt and in most cases will be more than enough to get any project up-and-running.

You can write webpages using any word processing program or text editor. There are also plenty of expensive programs (in the region of $200–$400) for making webpages. Rather than typing out the HTML tags yourself, you put together the various elements of the webpage by adding pictures and text as you would with a good word processor – you can then select text and change fonts, colours, sizes, etc., with the click of a button. The advantage of these tools is that they make webpage design more like word processing, something with which most teachers are familiar these days. The other advantage to these editors is that you can see exactly what the webpage will look like as you make it, without having to constantly look at it in a web browser.

Two of the best are: Dreamweaver from Adobe (http://www.adobe.com) and FrontPage from Microsoft (http://www.microsoft.com) – they both work very much like a word processor, but are quite complicated to learn. Free programs which take some of the hard work out of making webpages can be found on the Internet at the TUCOWS site (http://www.tucows.com) and of these I would recommend Arachnophilia.

When you have finished making a website, you need to put it onto the Internet for others to see. The easiest way of doing this is to use one of the free services for publishing websites on the Internet. There are many companies and websites which offer this service – check *Section 5* for more details.

Webpage making tips

1   Make sure you save all your files and images in the same place (directory or folder) on your hard disk. By doing this you can be sure that all the links you have made – and all the images you have added – will work properly.

2   Give your pages short, easily recalled names so that they can be easily identified, remembered and retrieved (ones with long difficult names often don't work!).

3   Don't use capital letters in filenames: they will work properly in Windows, but may not work on the Internet.

4   Plan your website on paper before you start making it. When you have a good structure, make a template and use it to make all the pages you need. Your template should be a simple 'model' page for your site, with all the common elements in it (navigation links, titles, etc.) – you can then copy this file each time you want to make a new page.

5   Spellcheck, proofread and test your site well before you make it available to the rest of the world. During testing, make sure all the links work properly, all the images display correctly and it looks how you expected it to look. For an example of a simple student website, see *Planning a website – Example: Our Class.*

When you have experimented with the basic guide to making webpages – and have put some pages on the Internet, you'll be ready to start working on the projects in this section. If you find that you want to learn more about making webpages, check the links in *Section 5*. Now let's move on to some sample projects.

TIP ☑

Don't forget that you can find sample templates (model pages) for these projects at the website which goes with this book. The templates are designed for easy editing from within a simple HTML editor like Netscape Composer. Visit http://www.cambridge.org/elt/chlt/internet for more information.

Sample projects

These are basic ideas for sample projects which lend themselves well to the medium of the webpage. These are just suggestions, and you should adapt the themes, content and site structure to suit your students.

LOCAL FOOD

This project aims to give people round the world the opportunity of getting to know the food of a particular country. The webpage might contain photographs of various dishes, sample menus from restaurants, a look at local ingredients, foodstuffs and wines. There is a mail link or small form for visitors to fill in. No recipes are given on the pages, but visitors are invited to write in and request recipes they're interested in. For a mixed nationality group, the page can focus on national dishes.

FESTIVALS

In this webpage project, students prepare descriptions of local festivals which happen throughout the year. This is a good example of an ongoing project. Every time a new festival comes along, students add it to their festival pages – descriptions, photographs, perhaps even sound or video. The photographs can be personal ones of the students and their families and friends involved in the various celebrations. Links to other sites on similar topics can also be added.

In this project, visitors are invited to write in with descriptions of festivals in their country or region, or simply to ask for more information on any of the festivals on the website itself. Again, for a mixed nationality class this can be limited to a look at the most important festival in each country represented.

> **TIP** ☑
>
> Business students can also benefit enormously from a webpage project. They can look at large company websites before going on to make a website for their company or business. Remember, most commerce on the Net is done in English, so this is an ideal opportunity for making a bilingual website. See *Section 5* for some good business sites.

IN THE NEWS

This project takes a look at local or national issues. Students make a mock-up of a newspaper featuring issues which are important in their country at the time of writing. This particular website invites questions and reactions from visitors and includes a 'write to the editor' page. For a collaborative project, try finding a school in another country and doing an international edition of the newspaper.

For mixed nationality classes, the newspaper can be modified to resemble a typical magazine which collects stories from around the world.

> **TIP** ☑
>
> You can find schools in other countries who are interested in email exchanges and collaborative projects by joining educational lists and mailing lists (see earlier in this section).
>
> Getting involved in a collaborative project is usually more rewarding for students since they have an immediate audience for their work. Added to this, a joint project provides plenty of opportunity for communication.

SQUARE EYES

What's the TV like where you live? This webpage focuses both on content and programming, and a look at personal preferences and viewing habits. Students provide a summary of a typical day's viewing where they live, coupled with their views on TV and a summary of their viewing habits.

Visitors are invited to write in to discuss programmes they have in common, talk about their viewing habits, ask about the quality of TV, etc.

WHAT'S THE STORY?

Students choose popular traditional stories from their country and put them up on the web. If possible these stories are also accompanied by drawings, information about the writers (if available), the setting, perhaps some historical or geographical background. The stories can be left unfinished, and visitors are invited to write in suggesting possible endings. These are posted up and voted on before the real endings are revealed.

THE BIG ISSUE

This website looks at an issue of local or national interest. The issue is explored in depth, considering the pros and cons and looking at possible solutions. You may decide that controversial issues such as abortion, drugs, divorce, etc., are more important than, for example, whether the local government should provide more parking space, but it is often the apparently trivial issues which fascinate people from other countries.

Encourage students to link their pages to other resources on the Net which feature similar information. Finally, add an email link or simple form for visitors to give their reactions, suggestions, etc.

THE BIG SCREEN

What are the big films of the moment? What sorts of films do students prefer, and who are their favourite actors and actresses? This website includes film reviews, statistics on cinema going habits, biographies of actors and actresses (with photos) and information on local stars. Visitors are invited to contribute with film reviews and opinions on film stars. The site could also include links to good film sites such as Hollywood.Com http://www.hollywood.com and the Internet Movie Database http://www.imdb.com

OUR CLASS

This is a big project looking at the entire class, the individuals, the teacher, activities in class, hobbies and interests outside class, the city or town, and the region. This website includes a photo of the class; clicking on a student takes the visitor to his/her page with personal information and a mail link. Visitors to the site are encouraged to write to the students and ask them

Planning a website – example: our class

In Class
The photo of the class is 'clickable' so that every student can have his/her own page.

In Class – Sample
This is the basic page for one of the students (Helena).

After School
Here the students and teacher explain what they like doing when they're not in class.

Out and About in. . .
A look at the region where the students live – what can you do there? Food, famous places . . .

Out and About in. . .
A look at the town where the students live.

This is a simple project which you will find at the website. Students work in groups to produce different sections, but also have the opportunity to express themselves individually on their personal page. The Write to Us link allows visitors to write and ask questions, leave comments, etc.

questions about their learning experiences, their hobbies, town, etc. A
variation of this project is one which focuses on the town or country.

LOCAL HEROES

Who are the famous people in the students' country – the national heroes
and heroines? This website has a gallery of famous people. Visitors can visit
different pages and find out about them all by reading biographies and
looking at photos, etc., including views by the students on which ones have
been most influential and why. There is an email link for visitors to write in
and give information about the heroes from their countries which are then
added to the 'And Also . . .' page. In multi-cultural classes, each nationality
represented can make a page about a hero or heroine from their country.

JUST FOR LAUGHS

What do people find funny? This website has views and opinions on humour,
a questionnaire to find out people's attitudes and a section for jokes and
funny stories. This would be an ideal opportunity for students to draw
illustrations for the jokes and stories and add them to the webpage. Visitors
are asked to give their opinions on what is and isn't funny, and to send in a
joke or story from their country.

TIP ☑

When you have finished a website and put it on the Internet, don't
forget to visit the major search engines to submit a link to your new
site. If it works, you'll get more visitors and more feedback. You'll find
links on the front pages of most search engines: look for options such
as *Submit a URL* or *Add a page*. Follow the link and fill in the form you
find there. If everything works properly, your page will be added to the
database.

Write to student and teacher mailing lists (see earlier in this section)
to encourage people to visit your site.

These are just a few examples of useful class projects. These can be done
both as stand-alone projects in a class, or as collaborative projects with other
schools and students around the world. The secret is to get students writing
and producing for the Internet, and to give them the opportunity to work
with other people and/or get interaction from the end-user of their work.

Project tips

1 Don't aim to produce anything which is beyond your own technical ability – fit the content to your skills to avoid problems during the production process.
2 Remember that the computer skills and time necessary to produce a finished product should not be so demanding as to detract from the language production. If students spend more time on – and have greater problems with – the technical aspects of a project, they will not benefit linguistically.
3 If collaborating on a project, fix a timetable of deadlines and responsibilities and make sure everyone sticks to them. It can be very frustrating for students to have to wait for a lazy partner.
4 Allow students to do as much of the decision-making and production as they can. This gives them a greater sense of ownership and responsibility for the project.

TIP ☑

If you don't have access to a lot of material for a particular project which interests your students, use the search skills you learnt in *Section 1* to find the material on the Internet. It is very important to check the copyright of anything you decide to use. For more information, see The Copyright Website which can be found at http://www.benedict.com or the numerous articles and opinions at the Electronic Freedom Foundation's site http://www.eff.org

---

4 Teacher Development

Section 4 of the book deals with teacher development online and with the growing area of online teaching itself. A book like this can only go some way to contributing to your developing technology skills, equipping you with a good set of techniques to get started. But what do you do next? The simple, quick and cheap answer is, of course, to look to the Internet for further development opportunities.

In this section we will be looking at online communities which deal with teacher training and development in technology, at a selection of opportunities for teaching online, and at a collection of resources to further your knowledge base.

4.1 Professional development online

There are plenty of opportunities for developing further once you have worked through the techniques and ideas in this book. These range from simple mailing lists, through Yahoo! Groups – which offer a wider range of services than simple email message exchanges – to Communities of Practice, which deal not only in the theory, but also (as their name suggests) with the practical applications of technology in the classroom.

Lists

Perhaps the easiest way to get something out of the Net is to learn from other people with more experience than yourself. Language teachers as a group were quick to realise the potential of the Net in their field of work, and have been working with it for over ten years. One excellent result of this long-term experience is that there are many thousands of teachers who are constantly in touch with each other, and sharing their experiences and resources with each other. The easiest way into this new world is to join a listserv.

Listservs are electronic mailing lists for specialist subjects. They are basically a collection of people interested in a particular subject or hobby who communicate with each other by email on a daily basis. All this communication is handled by a computer program which takes care of subscriptions, distributing the messages to subscribers and archiving past themes and discussions for future reference.

TESL-L

The most famous EFL related listserv is TESL-L (it stands for Teachers of English as a Second Language Listserv) and you can find it at listserv@cunyvm.cuny.edu It's based on a computer at the City University of New York in the US. This educational listserv has been running for many years, and has well over 30,000 members.

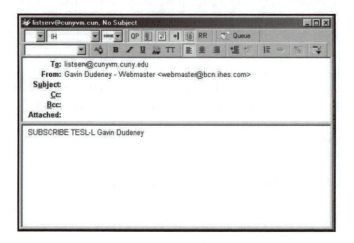

You join a listserv by sending an email message to a computer – you can see how to do this in the illustration above. When you send your subscription message to the listserv, remember that you're sending a message to a computer, and not to a person. Make sure that you put no information other than that which is required. If your subscription is successful you will receive a confirmation message within a short period of time. This confirmation message is very important – not only does it give you information about how the listserv works, but it also tells you what you can and can't do on the list. Read it carefully before you start to use the list.

TIP ☑

Listservs can generate a lot of messages on a daily basis if they are very popular. Don't subscribe to too many at the same time or you'll be overloaded with mail. If you find you do need to unsubscribe, send a message to the listserv as you did when you subscribed, changing the word 'subscribe' to 'unsubscribe'.

NETEACH-L

Another useful listserv is NETEACH-L, which is for teachers who use (or would like to use) the Internet in their teaching. It has over 10,000 subscribers and is a great place to start finding out how teachers are using Internet resources in their classes. Despite its name, you'll find that participants discuss all issues of technology in the classroom.

NETEACH-L works in the same way as TESL-L, the only difference being that no-one vets the messages – when you send one to the list it is automatically sent out to all the subscribers. This means that you have to think a little more carefully before sending the message in the first place, and make sure that you want all those people to see what you are writing, and that it's suitable for the list. For more information on NETEACH-L, visit http://hunter.listserv.cuny.edu/archives/neteach-l.html

These are just two of a list of thousands of listservs on many different subjects. For a full list of lists, visit L-Soft at http://www.lsoft.com/catalist.html where you will find an exhaustive database of Internet lists covering over 70,000 different fields including most major world languages.

Advantages of listservs

As far as language teachers are concerned, there really are a lot of benefits to be had from joining a listserv. Most of us have limited access to other teachers, teacher trainers, material and ideas, wherever we work. Joining a listserv effectively places us in the biggest 'teachers' room' in the world, with thousands of colleagues to talk to all the time.

A good reason for joining TESL-L specifically is that they have an enormous archive of past discussions and teacher resource files around various subjects built up over the years. These can be requested and received by email too, by using the *archive* facility.

TESL-L is also occasionally used as a medium for teaching. Quite recently it was possible to follow a course in Fluency First entirely taught by email. People who decided to do the course received ideas, lecture notes, pointers to books and materials, the possibility to chat with other students on the course and thus exchange ideas, experiences and suggestions.

If you have a special interest, these are also catered for in the TESL-L listserv. Once you have joined, you'll be able to take advantage of the smaller branches which range from English for Specific Purposes, through materials writers, a discussion of work conditions, CALL (Computer Assisted – or Aided – Language Learning), and many others.

Disadvantages of listservs

It's well known that you can't please all of the people all the time – and a listserv is no exception. A lot of the discussions will have no relevance to your own work most of the time. I particularly remember a debate about techniques used to remember Korean surnames in large classes, which – of course – was very useful for some of the subscribers, but of absolutely no relevance to me. Some people see this as a disadvantage, but try to look on a listserv as a magazine: there are always some articles you just don't want to read.

Of course, the more groups you join, the more mail you receive – this can lead to 'information overload', bigger phone bills and a great deal of irritation if you have to spend a lot of time every day downloading dozens of irrelevant messages. If after a while you find that you are no longer interested in being subscribed to this group, you can find instructions on how to unsubscribe in the original welcome message you were sent when you first subscribed – yet another good reason to hang on to it.

Using the listserv

Once you have subscribed and received your confirmation, you will also begin to receive email messages from other list subscribers. Let's take a look at how this works …

One member of the listserv in Japan (A) has suddenly been told she has to do a substitution class the following morning. It's an advanced level class (way above the level she is used to teaching) and she has no idea how to go about it. She sends an email message to the listserv asking for help. When the listserv receives the message, it automatically mails it to the 20,000 subscribers (B–E):

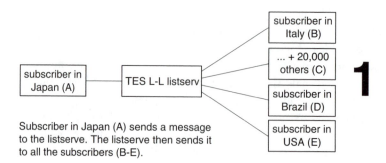

Subscriber in Japan (A) sends a message to the listserve. The listserve then sends it to all the subscribers (B-E).

Let's suppose a subscriber in Italy (B) has a great idea for the teacher in Japan. He can mail it directly to the teacher by using the email address in the teacher's original message:

Subscriber in Italy (B) replies directly to subscriber in Japan (A).

2

A subscriber in Brazil (D) has an idea which she thinks everyone might like to know about, so she sends her reply to the listserv which then sends it on to all the subscribers again. And so it goes on:

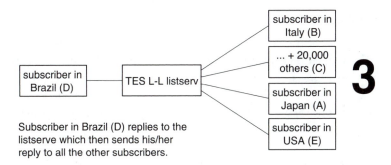

Subscriber in Brazil (D) replies to the listserve which then sends his/her reply to all the other subscribers.

3

It's not unusual for new subscribers to receive and read messages for just a short while, until they get the 'feel' of the listserv – this is known as 'lurking', and is considered part of getting to know a new group of people.

TESL-L generates a limited number of messages each day. This is because it is a moderated list, meaning that messages posted to the list are vetted before they go further than the main computer. Having said this, it can still generate a fair bit of mail on a daily basis. See *Listserv FAQs* for tips on how to control what you receive.

Student discussion lists

Student discussion lists are email mailing lists that have been set up specifically to allow students to contact each other and talk about subjects of mutual interest. These lists function in the same way as the teacher listservs above. Some example lists – all based at listserv@latrobe.edu.au – are:

BUSINESS-SL	Business and Economics
CHAT-SL	General conversation
DISCUSS-SL	Higher level conversation
EVENT-SL	Current Affairs
MOVIE-SL	Film and related themes
MUSIC-SL	Music and related themes
SCITECH-SL	Science and Technology
SPORT-SL	Sport and Games

These lists provide excellent opportunities for cross-cultural discussion between students. For more lists, see *Section 5*.

4.2 Listserv FAQs

DO I HAVE TO STAY CONNECTED ALL DAY TO
RECEIVE THE MESSAGES?

Listserv messages are written at all times of the day by people all around the world. If you don't want to (or can't) stay connected all day, set your subscription to *digest* format (you'll find instructions in your original welcome message). This way, all the messages of the day are put together into one longer email message and simply mailed to you once a day.

WHAT IF I'M NOT INTERESTED IN ALL THE MESSAGES?

Set your subscription to *index* format. In this format, all you receive is a list of the subject lines of the messages of the day. If you are interested in receiving any of the messages, you then send off for them. Again, instructions are included in the welcome message.

I'M GOING AWAY ON HOLIDAY AND I DON'T WANT TO
RETURN TO HUNDREDS OF EMAIL MESSAGES.
CAN I STOP THEM WHILE I'M AWAY?

Set your subscription to *nomail* when you plan to be away for a while. This will stop listserv messages being sent to you and clogging up your mailbox. When you return, you can set it to *mail* again.

HANDS ON 🖅

Subscribe to a couple of lists: one for professional purposes and one personal. (Use L-Soft – http://www.lsoft.com/catalist.html – to find lists which interest you.) Make sure you save the subscription confirmation and any rules and instructions you receive. Follow the discussions for a couple of days until you have a feel for the list, then send your first message. If after a while you find the list isn't helpful or useful to you, unsubscribe yourself.

Yahoo! groups

Another, more sophisticated, way of meeting other teachers online is to join one of the many Yahoo! Groups which bring teachers together to discuss teaching with technology. A Yahoo! Group generally functions like a mailing list, but incorporates more features.

Below is a screenshot of the IATEFL Learning Technologies Special Interest Group (SIG) Yahoo! Group at
http://groups.yahoo.com/group/LearningTechnologiesSIG/

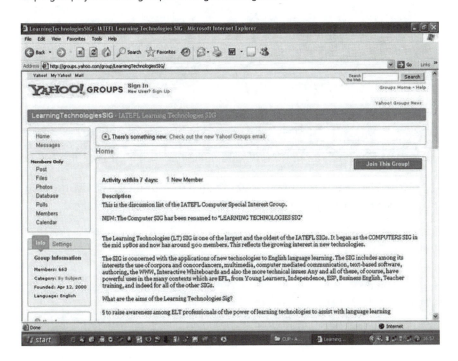

Essentially, a Yahoo! Group's basic function is to manage email communications (much like a listserv), but there is also a web-based interface giving access to more features. In the sample above, you can see that members get access to all the archives of the list, as well as files, photos, polls, a shared calendar, etc.

There are many such groups online, and it is best to get a Yahoo! ID for full access. To do this, visit the main page at http://groups.yahoo.com/ If you already have an ID, click on the *Sign In* button to proceed to the directory. If you need to sign up, click on the *Sign Up* link and follow the process through.

Once logged in as a member, you will see your groups on the left, and have full access to all the features of each group:

You can also search for more groups related to your interests. Use the *Find a Group* search box and enter a search term such as *ELT*:

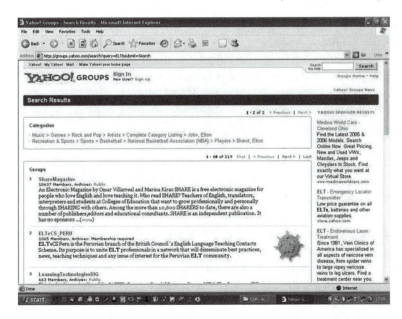

If you find a group that interests you, simply click on the title of the group to go to its homepage and then click on the blue *Join this Group*! button to join it.

Note that groups can be either moderated or unmoderated in terms of their postings – but they can also have moderated membership, and you may be invited to give a reason for wanting to join. These measures are usually in place to stop or limit undesirable members or unwanted advertising.

Once you are a member of a group, you will start to receive the messages by email. You can also go along to the webpage of each group for access to the other features. As with listservs, there are a few management options in terms of how you receive messages. To access your list management features, click on the *My Groups* link at the top of any of your subscribed group's pages. Once there, click on the *Edit my Groups* link:

From here you can manage your memberships, how you receive email, and other features.

It would be difficult to give an exhaustive list of relevant Yahoo! Groups, so judicious use of the search facility is recommended. One group which I would certainly recommend is Webheads in Action (http://groups.yahoo.com/group/evonline2002_webheads/), and we will be examining their work more closely in the section below.

Communities of Practice

To Etienne Wenger, a Xerox PARC researcher credited with coining the term, a Community of Practice (or CoP) is 'a group of people who share an interest in something, and come together to develop knowledge around this topic, in order to use it in practice'. A CoP contains three crucial elements: *knowledge domain* (the common topic binding the group together), *community* and *practice*. Membership of a CoP is ideally voluntary, the goals negotiated – normally in response to a commonly perceived need or problem.

In real life (f2f, or face-to-face situations) CoPs have had a natural tendency to develop, with groups of like-minded people drawn together in convenient meeting places at work or in social settings. However, pressures of modern life and the adoption of networked and distance communications have more recently given rise to the virtual equivalent – the distributed or online CoP. It is these groups which are increasingly being seen as a less threatening and more supportive environment for continuous professional development.

Online CoPs generally start as small websites, with members using various modes of communication and knowledge sharing – synchronous tools (such as chat, instant messaging or video-conferencing) or asynchronous tools (such as postings to bulletin boards or discussion lists) – as their preferred medium of interaction.

A well-functioning online CoP typically has a leader motivating the group and keeping it alive, and a group of core members contributing regularly to the group and keeping things ticking over. Then there are boundary members, who may contribute sporadically, or merely lurk, and perhaps belong to several online CoPs, thus transferring knowledge from one CoP to another (a boundary member may lurk on your CoP but be very active on another). Any CoP has a range of competencies which come to the fore depending on the area of expertise needed at any one point to help the group approach issues or problems. The structure of a CoP is attractively democratic in this sense: every member has potential value.

Online CoPs provide an excellent tool for professional development. For the EFL teacher, there are several well-established online CoPs, managed on a voluntary basis by the groups' founders. These go beyond the standard discussion list, with members actively trying out ideas and materials in their own classes, and in this sense are continually evolving their own creative practice.

One such group – Webheads in Action – is a long-established and thriving community of teachers interested in technology in the classroom. Set up by Vance Stevens, it not only provides the usual Yahoo! Group services, but also offers free online courses and training workshops, as well as the occasional online conference.

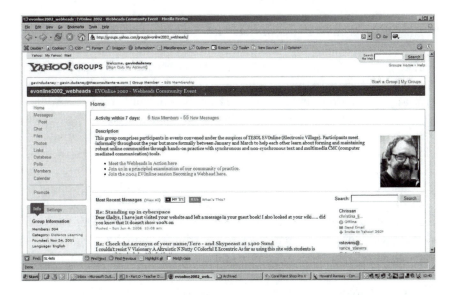

The group currently has over 500 members, with a wide range of skills from beginner to advanced, and as such is a very comfortable environment for any new member. Support is generously given, and they regularly run introductory sessions on how to get involved with the group. More

information on these sessions can be found here
http://groups.yahoo.com/group/becomingwebhead/ – this is the ideal way to get
started.

You can also find details of these training sessions and workshops on
Vance Steven's page at: http://www.geocities.com/vance_stevens/papers/
evonline2002/webheads.htm

It's worth remembering that it is the practical application of the shared
knowledge that is the main purpose of the group, and active involvement in
the work of the group is the best way of contributing to the shared
knowledge. This really is an excellent site to further your development in the
area.

4.3 Teaching online

So far in this book we have discussed one-off activities which can be used in
the classroom, but it is possible to take this a stage further and use the
Internet as the primary source of material for any given course.

Essentially this involves treating the Internet as a coursebook. This has
worked very well for me on courses which are not covered too well by
existing published materials, or where learners are on courses not leading to
'official' examinations. In Spain, where I was working until quite recently,
there is a large number of learners of English caught between the Cambridge
FCE and CAE examinations in a 'general advanced' level, and a relative
scarcity of printed materials of sufficient interest or novelty to cover their
needs.

By generating a syllabus and planning a course around the web, you can
easily prepare a useful, stimulating and rewarding study plan. Naturally the
search, evaluation and preparation skills you have picked up in this book
will help with this process, but it is worth bearing in mind that plenty of
materials have already been designed and are available online – from free
lesson plans to commercial sites with a wide variety of content.

Primary sources of materials are sites such as OneStopEnglish at
http://www.onestopenglish.com/ which features plenty of materials and lesson
plans for regular use. The BBC / British Council collaboration also has
plenty of resources on its Teaching English site at
http://www.teachingenglish.org.uk/ You may also want to check out the free
sections of iT's Online at http://www.its-online.com/

For more systematic online teaching, you can combine your own

materials with learner access to a site such as Macmillan English Campus at
http://www.macmillanenglishcampus.com/ allowing you to map the teaching
resources there to the coursebook or teaching materials you currently use
with your learners.

Other options in online resources include English To Go at
http://www.english-to-go.com/ and Flo-Joe (for Cambridge examination
preparation) at http://www.flo-joe.co.uk/

4.4 Teacher development resources

Here are a few sites, blogs and groups to get you started:

SITES
http://www.teachingenglish.org.uk/
http://www.iateflcompsig.org.uk/
http://dudeney.com/iatefl/ttedsig/
http://tdsig.free.fr/index.html
http://searchenglish.britishcouncil.org/
http://www.iatefl.org.pl/call/callnl.htm
http://www.languagesict.org.uk/default.htm
http://www.teachereducation.org.uk/
http://www.extremetechnoelt.com/moodle/index.php

BLOGS
http://www.ericbaber.com/blog/index.php
http://ictinelt.com/
http://janeknight.typepad.com/pick/
http://webquest.org/bdodge/index.htm
http://blog-efl.blogspot.com/
http://www.e-learningcentre.co.uk/eclipse/Resources/elblogs.htm

GROUPS
http://groups.yahoo.com/group/LearningTechnologiesSIG/
http://groups.yahoo.com/group/evonline2002_webheads/
http://groups.yahoo.com/group/dogme/
http://groups.yahoo.com/group/ict_and_english/
http://groups.yahoo.com/group/edutechsig/

5   **Websites**

Where can I publish my students' work?

These sites all offer free web space where you can host student work. (See *Section 3*.)

http://geocities.yahoo.com
http:// tripod.lycos.com
http://angelfire.lycos.com
http://www.bravenet.com
http://www.fortunecity.com

Where can I get email addresses for my students?

These sites offer free web-based email for your students. (See *Sections 2 and 3*.) They can be very slow and unreliable depending on the time of day and where in the world you are accessing them from. Their real disadvantage, however, is that they require you to be connected a lot of the time while you are reading and writing email. It's a good idea when working with sites like these to save messages to disk before disconnecting and reading them offline, as well as writing new messages before connecting and pasting them into the webmail message window.

http://mail.yahoo.com
http://www.hotmail.com
http://mail.lycos.com
http://webmail.netscape.com

Where can I get information about making webpages?

These sites offer advice on web design. (See *Section 3*.)

http://www.tucows.com
http://www.netscape.com
http://www.download.com
http://www.webmonkey.com
http://www.aitech.ac.jp/~iteslj/Articles/Kelly-MakePage/
http://hotpot.uvic.ca

Where can I find useful sites for teaching?

Here is a selection of sites I have found useful for dealing with various topics:

CALL

http://www.december.com/cmc/mag/index.html
http://www-writing.berkeley.edu/chorus/call/links.html
http://edvista.com/claire/call.html
http://www.iateflcompsig.org.uk/links.htm
http://www.eastment.com/links.html

Company / Business / ESP Pages

Most large companies have their own websites, and they are ideal for ESP classes. It would be pointless to include a list of such companies, but the best way to find them is to try the following: www.name_of_company.com for example, www.microsoft.com These are particularly useful for business vocabulary, simulations, etc.

The following addresses are all links to Business education sites:

http://www.besig.org
http://www.bized.ac.uk
http://www.eleaston.com/biz/bizhome.html
http://www.eslcafe.com/search/Business_English/
http://iteslj.org/links/TESL/Business_English/
http://www.eltweb.com

EFL/ESL/FLT

http://its-online.com
http://www.eslcafe.com
http://www.examenglish.com
http://www.englishtown.com
http://www.linguistic-funland.com
http://www.towerofenglish.com
http://www.esl-lab.com
http://www.englishlistening.com

History

http://www.thehistorychannel.co.uk/site/home/
http://www.nhm.ac.uk/
http://www.ed.gov/pubs/parents/History/Story.html
http://www.history.net
http://www.historyworld.net
http://www.historyofnations.net

Jobs

http://www.tefl.com/jobs/
http://eslemployment.com
http://www.eslcafe.com/joblist
http://englishjobmaze.com
http://www.eflteachingjobs.com
http://www.eslbase.com

Language / Reference

http://www.travlang.com/languages
http://humanities.uchicago.edu/forms_unrest/ROGET.html
http://www.m-w.com/netdict.htm
http://www.usingenglish.com/reference.html
http://dictionary.reference.com/
http://iteslj.org/links/ESL/Dictionaries_and_Reference_Materials/

Miscellaneous

http://movieweb.com/museum/main.html
http://www.encarta.msn.com/encartahome.asp
http://www.auschron.com/mrpants
http://www.guinnessrecords.com
http://www.britannica.com
http://www.bbc.co.uk

Movies

http://www.script-o-rama.com
http://www.oscar.com
http://www.hollywood.com
http://www.imdb.com
http://www.disney.com
http://www.cinema.com
http://www.film.com

Museums

http://www.nga.gov
http://wwar.com
http://www.yourwaytoflorence.com/uffizi/
http://www.nmsi.ac.uk/
http://www.si.edu
http://www.louvre.org

Music

http://www.mtv.com
http://www.rockhall.com
http://alwaysontherun.net
http://dir.yahoo.com/Entertainment/Music/
http://www.nme.com/
http://www.ubl.com/

News

http://www.news.yahoo.com
http://www.crayon.net
http://www.uttm.com
http://www.newsdirectory.com
http://www.newspapers.com
http://news.bbc.co.uk
http://www.cnn.com

Organisations

http://www.britcoun.org
http://www.iatefl.org
http://www.tesol.org/s_tesol/index.asp
http://www.calico.org
http://www.cal.org
http://www.philseflsupport.com/organisations.htm

Penpals

http://www.penpals.com
http://www.its-myworld.com/open/penpals.asp
http://www.arts.cuhk.edu.hk/~cmc/eltmatters/e-mail.htm
http://www.wfi.fr/volterre/keypals.html
http://iteslj.org/links/ESL/Penpals_and_Communicating_with_Others/
http://www.vcu.edu/cspweb/,icp/ppadvice.html

Politics / Government

http://www.parliament.uk
http://www.royal.gov.uk
http://www.open.gov.uk
http://www.whitehouse.gov
http://www.foe.co.uk/
http://www.greenpeace.org/

Search pages

http://www.yahoo.com
http://www.google.com
http://search.looksmart.com
http://www.lycos.com
http://www.ask.com
http://www.go.com

Sport

http://www.nba.com
http://www.ioc.org
http://www.sportsnetwork.com/
http://www.pecentral.org/websites/sportsites.html
http://news.bbc.co.uk/sport1/hi/academy/default.stm
http://espn.go.com/

Student writing

http://darkwing.uoregon.edu/~leslieob/pizzaz.html
http://www.otan.us/webfarm/emailproject/email.htm
http://www.teachingenglish.org.uk/think/resources/blogging.shtml
http://www.ohiou.edu/esl/english/writing/index.html
http://www.powa.org/
http://www.kidpub.org/kidpub/

Travel and tourism

http://www.travlang.com/languages
http://www.ukguide.org/index.html
http://www.hm-usa.com/index.html
http://www.galenfrysinger.com/index.htm
http://www.travelpod.com/
http://www.bluebear.com.au/travel/

Younger learners

http://www.bonus.com
http://www.ajkids.com
http://yahooligans.yahoo.com
http://www.youngcommonwealth.org
http://www.thepotters.com/puzzles/kids.html
http://www.countryschool.com/younglearners.htm

Glossary

There's a lot of jargon involved in using the Internet. This short list covers the main terms which come up in this book and introduces some other common ones which you're likely to encounter when on the Net.

ADSL	A fast Net connection which is always on.
Application	A piece of software that performs a useful function.
Archive	A file (or files) that have been compressed to form one smaller file. Software distributed on the Net is usually archived.
Attachment	A file sent together with an email message. (See *Section 1*.)
Blog	A diary on the Internet – a web log. (See *Section 3*.)
Bookmark	A way of saving a web address for future reference (also called Favorites). (See *Section 1*.)
Bounce	When email is returned due to a delivery failure. (See *Section 1*.)
Browser	A program like Internet Explorer or Firefox which displays webpages. (See *Section 1*.)
Cache	Recently visited webpages stored on your computer. (See *Section 1*.)
CALL	Computer Assisted (or Aided) Language Learning. (See also TELL.)
Chat	The part of the Internet used to communicate in real time by typing messages to one or more other people. (See *Section 4*.)
Cross post	To send the same message to more than one list or newsgroup.
Dial-up	To connect to the Net using a computer modem and phone line.
Download	The transfer of a file from one computer to another over the Net.
Email	Electronic Mail. A method of sending messages via computer. (See *Section 1*.)

Emoticons (also Smilies)	A facial expression made using punctuation, e.g. :-) These are used in email and chat to communicate feelings or emotions. They must be viewed sideways to get the full effect.
Encryption	A method of coding information to prevent unauthorised access. Most common in online shopping for sending credit card details.
FAQ	Frequently Asked Questions. You will find FAQs all over the Net. Their purpose is to provide easy access to the most common questions related to an issue.
FTP	File Transfer Protocol. A method of transferring files from one computer to another.
Hardware	The physical components of a computer: screen, monitor, etc.
Homepage	The main page of a website. (See *Section 1*.)
Host	A computer which holds information on the Internet. Most commonly seen in browser error message: *Host Not Found*.
HTML	Hypertext Mark-Up Language. The language used to write a web document. (See *Section 3*.)
ISP	Internet Service Provider. The company which helps you to connect to the Internet . (See *Section 1*.)
Link	A piece of text or image on a webpage which, when clicked on, takes the user to another page or website. (See *Section 1*.)
LISTSERV	An automated mailing list distribution system. (See *Section 4*.)
Lurking	Subscribing to a listserv or newsgroup but not participating.
Mailing list	An automated email system similar to a listserv.
Modem	A piece of hardware which allows two or more computers to communicate with each other using normal phone lines. (See *Section 1*.)
Netiquette	The etiquette of Internet usage. (See *Section 1*.)
Newbie	A newcomer to the Internet – used as a term of ridicule.
Newsgroup	A message area defined by subject matter. There are over 120,000 newsgroups. Similar to listservs and mailing lists, they are usually more 'anarchic' in

content. Software called a newsreader is needed to
subscribe to and read newsgroups.

Shareware
Software which is generally available in a try-before-
you-buy form.

Software
Programs installed and run on a computer.

Spam
An unsolicited email message sent to lots of people.

TELL
Technology Enhanced Language Learning. This
covers all aspects of using technology in language
instruction, as opposed to the more limited field of
CALL which refers exclusively to the use of
computers.

Video-conferencing
A form of audio-visual communication on the
Internet. You need a video camera, sound card and a
fast Internet connection.

Webpage
One screen of information on the Internet. (See
Section 1.)

Website
A collection of webpages built around a common
theme. (See *Section 1*.)

World Wide Web
A hypertext information and resource system for the
Internet. (See *Section 1*.)

Appendix A – Website Review Form

GENERAL INFORMATION	
Name of site:	
URL of site:	
Date visited:	
Reviewer:	

SITE SUMMARY	
Description Add a short description of the site	
Content summary Give a brief summary of the contents of the site	

SITE DETAILS	
Information Is the site content correct, reliable and accurate? Is the writer an expert in this subject?	
Currency Is the site up-to-date? When was new information last added? When were the pages last updated?	
Content Is the content interesting, relevant, funny, useful or entertaining? How would you describe it?	
Presentation Is it attractive and easy to navigate? Does it use a lot of graphics, sound or multimedia files?	
Functionality Does it all work? Are there any broken links or missing pages? Does it take a long time to display pages?	

VERDICT	
	Excellent ( ) Very good ( ) Good ( ) Average ( ) Poor ( )

© Cambridge University Press 2007

Appendix B – Student Release Form

STUDENT INFORMATION	
Name:	....
Address:	....
	....
	....
Tel. no:	....

PROJECT INFORMATION	
School or institution:	....
Project description:	....
Release details:	....
	....
	....
	....
	NOTE: Specify if the student's work can be used for general publishing, school or institution publicity, etc.

AUTHORISATION	
For the student:	Signature: ....
	Name: ....
	Note: If the student is under 18, this form must be signed by a parent or legal guardian.
On behalf of the school:	Signature: ....
	Name: ....
Date:	....

Appendix B is a sample release form for students to sign, giving the school or institution permission to use their work on the website. This constitutes a basic agreement between the student and the school, in which the student agrees to allow written material produced by them to be published on the website without the problem of copyright cropping up. It's a good idea to find out if any students are likely to have a problem with their work being published on the Internet before starting work on a project. Any form of this nature cannot take into account local conditions and regulations, so this should be taken as a simple suggestion only.

References

Barrett, B. and Sharma, P. (2003) *The Internet and Business English*, Summertown Publishing.

Darby, J. and Joyce, M. (July 1995) 'Using the Internet for Teaching', *Active Learning 2*.

Eastment, D. (April 1996) 'The Internet for Teachers and Learners', *Modern English Teacher*, 5,2.

Eastment, D., Hardisty, D. and Windeatt, S. (2000) *The Internet*, Oxford University Press.

Lewis, G. (2004) *The Internet and Young Learners*, Oxford University Press.

Motteram, G. (February 1996) 'The Internet for ELT: A newbie's guide', *IATEFL Newsletter*.

Sperling, D. (1997) *The Internet Guide for English Language Teachers*, Prentice-Hall.

Sperling, D. (1998) *Dave Sperling's Internet Guide*, Prentice-Hall.

Sperling, D. (1999) *Dave Sperling's Internet Activity Workbook*, Prentice-Hall.

Teeler, D. and Gray, P. (2000) *How to Use the Internet in ELT*, Longman.

Warschauer, M. (1995) *E-mail for English teaching*, TESOL.

Index

Note: References in **bold** refer to the Glossary; those in *italic* to illustrations.